Shrubs for South Dakota

Contents

Shrubs for South Dakota

John Ball
Associate Professor, Arboriculture/Urban Forestry
Horticulture, Forestry, Landscape and Parks Department

David F. Graper
Extension Horticulture Specialist
Horticulture, Forestry, Landscape and Parks Department

Carol M. F. Wake
Assistant Professor, Biology/Microbiology Department

Photographs and botanical drawings by John Ball

Shrubs are an essential part of any South Dakota residential landscape, providing an attractive setting for our homes and colorful backdrops to our perennial beds and borders.

Spring-flowering shrubs help us forget the gloom of winter, while summer flowers and fall fruit and foliage add beauty to what seems a too-short outdoor season. Shrubs, however, are more than just landscape ornaments. They provide food and shelter for wildlife. They can be living snowfences and windbreaks. And if we come to sell our homes, we find an attractive landscape that includes shrubs has added economic value to our properties.

This book is divided into five main sections: Deciduous and Broadleaf Evergreen Shrubs, Vines, Conifer Shrubs, a List of Plants With Adaptive or Ornamental Characteristics, and a Summer Key to Shrubs. The first three sections provide descriptions of the many shrubs that can grow in South Dakota and provide pictures and growing information. The plants in each section are arranged alphabetically by botanical names, rather than by common names, since most shrubs have more than one common name but all have only a single botanical name. We have used the most frequently used common names for each of the shrubs and Lakota names, when known, for native shrubs.

This book is a useful guide to shrubs in the Northern Plains. It does not, however, cover every possible shrub that might survive somewhere in South Dakota, since the number of shrubs or cultivars that can grow here, particularly in the southeastern part of our state, can be numbered in the hundreds. The most common species and cultivars that you might find at a South Dakota garden center or nursery are included.

The list of adapted shrubs expands every year as new cultivars are introduced. Just because a species or cultivar does not appear in this book, do not assume it cannot grow here. It may be a new or rare cultivar. Consult with your local garden center, landscape nursery, or landscape or tree care company to see if the plant in question might be acceptable. Above all else, experiment. If it were not for the many avid gardeners who decided to try something new, we would not know what could grow in the various regions of our state.

SHRUB NAMES

Each page begins with common names for the plant or plants in the same genus. A genus (pl. genera) is a group of closely related plants. Usually, they have similar flower and fruiting characteristics. Beneath the common names for the genus are the common and botanical names for all the species within the genus that are covered in this book. If the species is native to the state, the Lakota name is also given, if known.

Common names are taken from various sources. *The Manual of Woody Landscape Plants: Their Identification, Ornamental Characteristics, Culture, Propagation and Uses*, 4th ed, by Michael Dirr (Stipes Publishing Company, Champaign, IL, 1990) is the most frequent source.   Lakota names are taken from *Lakota Names and Traditional Uses of Native Plants by Sicangu (Brule) People in the Rosebud Area, South Dakota* by Dilwyn J. Rogers (Rosebud Educational Society, Inc., St. Francis, SD, 1980).

PLANTING REGIONS

South Dakota is an extremely diverse state with a wide range of different soils and climates.   Predicting how a given shrub species will perform in a particular region is difficult as different cultivars of a species may not be equally adaptable.

For example, the Brandon arborvitae (*Thuja occidentalis* 'Brandon') can be successfully grown throughout East River and much of the Black Hills. But the Holmstrup arborvitae (*T. occidentalis* 'Holmstrup'), a different cultivar of the same species, is limited to the southeastern portion of our state. Likewise, closely related species, such as the viburnums, may have widely different growing requirements.

The accompanying map divides the state into eight major ecological regions, each with its own unique soils, topography, precipitation patterns, average summer and winter temperatures, and natural vegetation. A recommended region offers favorable growing conditions for the species and is usually a reliable spot for any of its cultivars. Adjacent

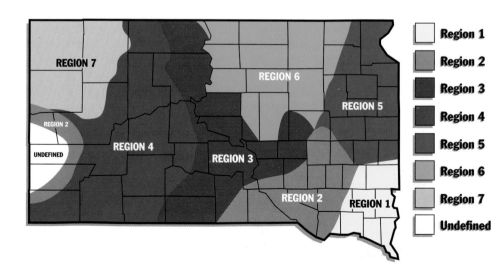

Shrubs for South Dakota

regions should be considered marginal for good performance; in protected sites or with supplemental irrigation, the shrub may do well, but generally its performance will not be as good as in more favorable locations. Cultivars should also be selected more carefully as some may not be able to grow in the less favorable conditions. Regions not mentioned are those where the growth or survival of the species and its cultivars is in doubt. In highly protected sites, with additional care, the plant may survive.

While changes from one region to another may appear abrupt, the changes are actually much more gradual. Individuals living near the border of two regions may want to use the more conservative recommendation to be better assured of success.

GUIDE TO ICONS

Ornamental features

Icons indicate some of the desirable characteristics and growing requirements of the group of plants. Again, these are only general guides; individual species and their cultivars may have slightly different ornamental features and growing requirements. The icons will make you aware of the landscape potential of each plant. You will need to read farther into the descriptions to determine if a particular species or cultivar has the features that you desire.

Attractive attributes. Every shrub has at least one attribute that makes it a desirable ornamental plant. It may have attractive flowers, interesting fruit, brilliant fall foliage color, or unique bark. Many of our better ornamental shrubs have several attributes.

On each page there will be icons to denote attractive attributes that may be found in the genus. This does not mean that every plant or cultivar listed on the page has all the attributes identified, just that they are possibilities, depending upon species and cultivar selection.

 leaves with summer or fall color   *showy flowers*

 unique bark   *attractive fruit*

Shape. A silhouette of the typical form of the species is provided for each of the plants in this book. Cultivars may have a different shape than the species. In fact, for some cultivars, unique shapes are their ornamental value.

Globe   *Arching*   *Upright/pyramidal*   *Vine*

Spreading   *Tree-like*   *Groundcover*

Size. Shrub size is included in the text and is only a rough approximation of size at maturity. Mature plant size is influenced by many factors including climate, soil, and shading. A plant may not grow to the size given, particularly in unfavorable planting regions.

 Wildlife value. Many of our shrubs have seeds or fruit that are attractive and beneficial to wildlife. Many also provide dense nesting cover. The bird icon identifies those groups of plants that are especially attractive to birds and other wildlife.

 Deer damage. While most homeowners appreciate wildlife as desirable additions to the landscape, many want and need to discourage deer from feeding in their yards.

There are no "deer-proof plants." Any shrub will be damaged if a 100- to 200-pound animal lies on it or uses it to preen antlers. Also, almost any shrub will be browsed under starvation conditions.

Shrubs in this book identified by the deer symbol are less desirable to deer under normal conditions. However, if one shrub is identified by a deer symbol, do not assume other members of the same genus are equally resistant. Closely related plants may vary greatly in their attractiveness to deer. Common juniper, for example, is rarely browsed upon, while Rocky Mountain juniper is a preferred food source.

Environmental requirements

Tolerance of alkaline soils. These icons indicate the shrub's ability to tolerate alkaline soils, those soils with a pH greater than 7.0. Almost all shrubs perform best in a soil that is slightly acidic (pH 6.2 - 6.8), but many will tolerate some degree of alkalinity and a few shrubs even perform better. If the box is shaded in **green**, the shrub is very tolerant to alkaline soils and can be planted in soils with a pH in excess of 7.5. If the box is **yellow**, the plant will accept slightly alkaline soils but should not be planted in soils with a pH above 7.5. If the box is **red**, the plant will not tolerate alkaline soils and should be planted in a soil with a pH less than 7.0 and preferably less than 6.2. If shrubs that are not tolerant of alkaline soils are planted in high-pH soils, the foliage usually becomes chlorotic.

Alkaline tolerant   *Alkaline slightly tolerant*   *Alkaline intolerant*

Tolerance of shade. Many shrubs are planted beneath trees or in the shade of buildings. If they are not shade tolerant, they may produce few flowers and fruit, become very open, and may even die. If the box shows a **full sun**, the shrub requires full sun for most of the day. If the box shows a **half sun**, the plant can tolerate part sun, meaning at least a half day of direct sunlight or filtered sunlight throughout the day. If the box shows a **darkened sun**, the shrub can grow in shade. Most ornamental shrubs do best in full sun; even if they tolerate shade they may produce fewer flowers and be slightly more open if planted in shade.

Shade tolerance refers to shade during the growing season. Some evergreens require winter shade to prevent or reduce winter-burn.

Sun

Part-sun

Shade

Cultural requirements

Pruning needs. Most shrubs require occasional pruning to look their best. If the box shows a plant **with leaves (green)**, the shrub should be pruned after it flowers since its flower buds are formed the previous growing season. If the box shows a plant **without leaves (brown)**, the shrub should be pruned during the dormant season as its flower buds are set during the growing season. For more information on how to properly prune shrubs, see *Extension Extra 6033, Pruning Deciduous Shrubs.*

Prune after flowering

Prune during dormant season

Evergreen shrub pruning is covered in the conifer evergreen section.

A FINAL NOTE. You'll find occasional reference to the writing of N.E. Hansen and other early horticulturists in South Dakota. Professor Hansen served in the Horticulture Department at the then South Dakota State College from 1895 to 1937, making numerous trips throughout Europe and Asia to collect plants to bring back to the Northern Plains. His writings on the characteristics and growing requirements of many shrubs in this book are as valuable now as they were when first written. We think you'll appreciate his thoughts and opinions as well as those of other pioneer horticulturists. Without their efforts our ornamental landscapes would be much diminished. This book is dedicated to these men and women.

Deciduous and Broadleaf Evergreen Shrubs for South Dakota

The following section is devoted to the many deciduous shrubs available to the South Dakota gardener and also includes evergreen or semi-evergreen shrubs (i.e. boxwood, daphne, and others) that are not conifers. The conifers, including the arborvitaes, junipers, yews, and dwarf spruce and pines, are in a separate section of this book.

Flowering times

The key to an appealing ornamental landscape is to have a sequence of blooms throughout the growing season. Many gardeners, enticed by the riot of colors after a gray and white winter, buy all their plants in bloom during their spring trip to the local garden center. This results in a landscape that is overpowering in May but almost lifeless the remainder of the year.

The following chart gives the sequence of flowering for many of our most popular shrubs. The dates are approximate; actual date of bloom depends upon how soon warm weather begins in the spring. For example, pagoda dogwood in Brookings may begin blooming as early as May 15 or as late as June 16, depending upon the spring weather. However, its place in the sequence of flowering will remain about the same.

Some of these plants may not occur in your particular area and obviously, the bloom sequence will begin earlier in Yankton than it will in Bison. Most flowering shrubs will remain in bloom from 3 days to 2 weeks depending upon weather conditions. Shrubs that have an extended floral display have that period identified by a dotted line.

Forsythia
 Buffaloberry
  Bridalweath spirea
   P. J. M. rhododendron
    Serviceberry
     Garland spirea
     Siberian peashrub
     Hyacinth lilac
     Fragrant sumac
     Clove currant
      Creeping mahonia
       Wayfaringtree
       Scarlet elder
       Common lilac
        Lights series azaleas
        Korean barberry
         Japanese barberry
         Koreanspice viburnum
             Weigela ···
              Chokeberry
             Purpleleaf sandcherry
              Potentilla ···
               Rose-acacia ···
              Daphne
               Redoiser dogwood
               Tatarian honeysuckle
                Vanhoutte spirea
                 Nippon spirea
                 European fly honeysuckle
                  Chinese lilac
                   Sakhalin honeysuckle
                    Dwarf Korean lilac
                    Manchurian lilac
                   Nannyberry
                     European cranberrybush
                     Ninebark
                      Downy arrowwood
                       American cranberrybush
                      Preston lilac
                       Sargent viburnum ··········
                        Tatarian dogwood ·································
                        Japanese spirea ··
                        Arrowwood
                        Mockorange
                         Bumalda spirea ·································
                        Smokebush
                          Ural falsespirea ·······································
                          Elderberry
                          Dwarf bush-honeysuckle ·······················
                           White snowberry
                            Panicle hydrangea ················
                           Trumpetvine
                            Hill-of-snow hydrangea ····················
                             Smooth sumac
                              Chenault coralberry
                               Coralberry
                                Butterfly bush ···························
                                Tamarisk

May   *June*   *July*   *August*

Fiveleaf aralia

Fiveleaf aralia   *Acanthopanax sieboldianus*   Region 1,2,5

Fiveleaf aralia is an old-fashioned favorite that is being "rediscovered." Its primary ornamental value comes from its unique fruit and its ability to survive in tough locations. The fruit, which forms in late summer, is a black berry about ¼ inch in diameter. Berries occur in clusters. The greenish-white flowers are not particularly showy, nor is there any fall color although the green foliage persists into winter. The plant has small thorns and, because of its dense branching, can serve as a barrier. Fiveleaf aralia reaches a height and spread of 6 to 8 feet. The plant often will sucker at the base. The best use for this shrub is as a mass planting or a screen.

Fiveleaf aralia is adaptable to a wide range of soils, particularly those that are dry. It will tolerate alkaline soils and full sun to dense shade. The primary drawback is its limited hardiness for many areas of the state where it may die back to the ground each winter.

Acanthopanax sieboldianus

Deciduous and Broadleaf Evergreen Shrubs

Juneberry, Saskatoon, Serviceberry, Shadblow, Sugarberry

Saskatoon serviceberry	*Amelanchier alnifolia*	Region 1,2,3,5,6
Allegheny serviceberry	*Amelanchier laevis*	Region 1,2,3,5
Apple serviceberry	*Amelanchier* x *grandiflora*	Region 1,2,3,5

Wipazutkan is the Lakota name for the saskatoon serviceberry.

Serviceberries have outstanding ornamental characteristics; they have truly four seasons of interest. In the spring before the leaves appear, the plant is covered with white, 5-petaled flowers. The flowers generally last a week but the bloom period can be as brief as 3 days.

Amelanchier x grandiflora

The names juneberry and sugarberry all refer to the sweet fruit which typically ripens in June. Beginning in the early summer, the shrub produces an abundant crop of small, red to bluish fruits to which birds take readily. In the fall, the leaves turn a bright apricot-orange to a dusty red, and during the winter the smooth, bluish-gray bark stands out against the snow cover.

The name serviceberry comes from the fact that the trees flower early in the spring, about the time northern communities conducted burial services for the people that died during the winter. The shad, a common New England fish, often begin their run up the rivers at the time of bloom.

While all serviceberries have similar ornamental characters, they differ greatly in mature size and form. Allegeny serviceberry becomes a small tree that often reaches a height of 20 feet. It generally occurs as a multiple-stemmed tree so the spread can equal the height. The apple serviceberry can be as tall as the Allegeny. The apple serviceberry's primary difference is in the flowers; they are larger and have a pink tinge when they first open. The Saskatoon serviceberry is a medium- to large-sized shrub achieving a height anywhere from 5 to 12 feet. The spread is equally variable. The plant will also sucker.

Amelanchier x grandiflora

All serviceberries are adaptable to full-sun and shade locations. They do best on slightly acid to neutral soils that are well drained. The plants have few serious pest problems in South Dakota. The most common problem is powdery mildew.

The most common cultivars are two apple serviceberries: 'Robin Hill' with pink flowers in the bud stage and 'Autumn Brilliance' known for its outstanding brilliantly red-orange fall color. 'Regent' is a cultivar of Saskatoon serviceberry that has excellent fruit. It has a mature height and spread of 4 to 6 feet.

Saskatoon serviceberry is native to woody draws in much of South Dakota and was an important part of the Lakota diet. *Wipazuka waste wi* means "good juneberry moon," referring to June as a time when the serviceberry fruit becomes ripe. The fruit was eaten fresh and was extensively dried for winter storage. The fruit was pounded into patties and sun-dried. Meriweather Lewis, in his journal of the Lewis and Clark expedition, mentions serviceberry patties that weighed as much as 10 pounds. The dried berry was used as an ingredient in pemmican. The fruit is still enjoyed by many as it makes excellent jams, pies, and wine and is a delicious addition to pancakes and muffins.

Chokeberry

Black chokeberry	*Aronia melanocarpa*	Region 1,2,3,5,6
Red chokeberry	*Aronia arbutifolia*	Region 1,2
Purple chokeberry	*Aronia prunifolia*	Region 1,2,3,5

Chokeberries, not to be confused with chokecherry, are an attractive but often overlooked group of ornamental plants, rated among the top 10 ornamental shrubs for the upper Midwest by many gardening authorities. The high rating comes from having three distinct seasons of interest. Chokeberries have white 5-petaled flowers in the spring that occur in flat-shaped clusters of 10 or more individual flowers. This is followed in mid-summer by clusters of ⅓- to ½-inch diameter fruit. The fruit is persistent and will often remain attached to the twigs until late spring when they are taken by birds. The fruit can be used for juice or mixed with other juices as an extender. The fall foliage is a dark purplish-red.

There are three species of chokeberry—red, black, and purple—along with several cultivars of each. The main differences among the species are in winter hardiness and fruit color. As the common names indicate, red chokeberry has bright red fruit, black chokeberry has shiny black fruit, and the purple chokeberry has shiny purplish-black fruit. The hardiest one of the three is black chokeberry, followed by the purple and then the red.

Aronia melanocarpa

The black chokeberry was termed a "promising ornamental shrub" by N.E. Hansen in the 1930s. This is the species that is best adaptable to the South Dakota climate. Red chokeberry is a possibility in protected locations.

The three also differ in mature height and spread. Red chokeberry has an upright form and can reach a height of 8 feet and a spread of 5 feet. Black chokeberry is more rounded with a height and spread of 5 to 6 feet. Purple chokeberry is the largest of the three with a mature height of 10 feet or more and a spread of 5 to 8 feet. All three species sucker profusely and often tend to have less foliage near the base. Because of these two characteristics, the plants are best suited to borders and mass plantings where they are superior choices.

Chokeberries are adaptable to a wide range of soils from sandy loam to clay loam. They may, however, become chlorotic on soils with a pH above 7.5. They have few pest problems.

Aronia melanocarpa

There are two noteworthy cultivars of chokeberry: 'Brilliantissima,' a cultivar of red chokeberry with a deep red fall color, and 'Autumn Magic,' a cultivar of black chokeberry with red and purple fall color.

Barberry

Korean barberry	*Berberis koreana*	Region 1,2,3,5
Mentor barberry	*Berberis* x *mentorensis*	Region 1,2
Japanese barberry	*Berberis thunbergii*	Region 1-7

Barberries are a group of plants noted for their use as dense, thorny barriers. However, they have much more value than this in the ornamental landscape. Depending upon the species and particular cultivar selected, the plant may have attractive flowers, interesting fruit, and colorful foliage.

Korean barberry has showy yellow flowers that hang from the branches in the spring. This is followed in the late summer by bright red ¼-inch fruit that hangs in clusters and often persists into the winter. In the fall, the foliage turns a deep purplish-red. Korean barberry may reach a height of 5 feet with an equal spread. It also suckers profusely so it can form large masses in time.

The Japanese barberry is the most common barberry in the landscape. The flowers are not showy; however, the ⅓-inch long bright red fruit persists through the winter. The greatest ornamental feature of the Japanese barberry is the multitude of foliage colors available, primarily in cultivars of *B. thun-*

Berberis koreana

Shrubs for South Dakota

Berberis thunbergii

bergii var. *atropurpurea*. The colors range from the variegated rose-red of 'Rosy Glow' to the reddish-purple of 'Bailone.' Fall color can also be attractive, ranging from a scarlet-orange to a burgundy-purple depending upon the cultivar. Japanese barberry generally has a rounded, compact form and reaches a height between 2 to 5 feet depending upon the cultivar.

There is also a hybrid between Japanese and Korean barberry called 'Emerald Carousel' (*Berberis* 'Tara'). Its summer foliage is deep green, turning reddish purple in the fall. Foliage is retained late into the year. The plant is dense and rounded, about 4 to 5 feet tall, and with an equal spread.

Mentor barberry is a semi-evergreen barberry which can maintain much of its foliage through the winter. The foliage is green during the summer and turns dull red in the fall. It is a large plant with a potential height and spread of 5 feet. It is not reliably hardy in much of South Dakota but may survive in protected locations in the southeastern part of our state.

Barberries are excellent barrier plants because of their thorns and dense growth; however, they can also make excellent hedges and accent plants. Barberries are very adaptable, tolerating most (except wet) soil conditions. Japanese barberry will tolerate soil with a pH above 7.5.

Barberries do best in full sun, though Korean barberry will tolerate part sun. Barberries have few pest problems, but they do require annual pruning to look their best. Some barberry species, such as common barberry (*B. vulgaris*), serve as alternate hosts for the black stem rust of wheat. Japanese, Korean, and Mentor barberry and their cultivars are not alternate hosts and are safe to plant in wheat growing regions.

Butterfly bush, Summer-lilac

Butterfly bush   *Buddleia davidii*   Region 1,2

Butterfly bush is a woody plant that is better treated as a herbaceous perennial. The top is not winter-hardy, so the plant will die back to the ground during most South Dakota winters. However, this should not eliminate it from consideration, as butterfly bush flowers on new wood and is a vigorous sprouter. Flowering is reliable in our state and the plant deserves a spot in our landscapes. The white or red to purple flowers occur in large spikes from mid-summer to fall, are very fragrant, and attract butterflies. They may also be cut and dried for arrangements.

Butterfly bush is multiple-stemmed and will reach a summer height of about 3 feet with a wider spread. It does best in full sun and on fertile, well-drained soils. It should be pruned to 4 or 5 inches after the winter.

Buddleia davidii

Box, Boxwood

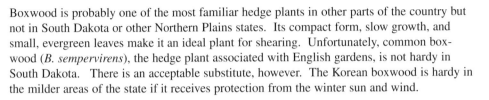

Korean boxwood   *Buxus microphylla* var. *koreana*   Region 1,2,5

Boxwood is probably one of the most familiar hedge plants in other parts of the country but not in South Dakota or other Northern Plains states. Its compact form, slow growth, and small, evergreen leaves make it an ideal plant for shearing. Unfortunately, common boxwood (*B. sempervirens*), the hedge plant associated with English gardens, is not hardy in South Dakota. There is an acceptable substitute, however. The Korean boxwood is hardy in the milder areas of the state if it receives protection from the winter sun and wind.

Korean boxwood's spring flowers are not showy but are sweetly fragrant. Fruits are also not very showy. Evergreen foliage and compact growth are the plant's primary ornamental features. The foliage may turn yellowish-green during the winter. 'Wintergreen' is the only cultivar to maintain green foliage in the winter.

Korean boxwood may reach a height of 4 feet with a slightly smaller spread. Boxwood does best in full sun, but it is often necessary to plant in shade so that the evergreen foliage has winter shading to avoid winter-burn. The roots require a cool, moist soil, so mulching is also beneficial. The plant suffers few problems other than surviving our winters.

Buxus microphylla var. *koreana*

Caragana, Peashrub, Siberian peashrub

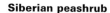

Siberian peashrub   *Caragana arborescens*   Region 1-7

Siberian peashrub is a common hedge or windbreak shrub in South Dakota. N.E. Hansen called it "the best plant for hedges, low windbreaks, and snowcatchers for the prairie." He was so taken by this Siberian plant that he brought back more than 350 pounds of seed from an 1897 collection trip to Russia.

Caragana arborescens

Peashrub has yellow, pea-like flowers in the spring, usually opening when the leaves have almost fully expanded, so the flowers are somewhat hidden by the leaves. The fruit is a small pod that forms in late summer and remains on the shrub until fall. Fall color is at best yellowish-green.

Siberian peashrub can reach a height of 12 feet with an equal spread.

There are two very interesting weeping cultivars available. 'Pendula' and 'Walker' have single stems on top of which the weeping form is grafted. Both cultivars are about 4 or 5 feet tall with a spread of 3 feet. The primary difference between the two is that 'Walker' has a more pronounced weeping form.

Some other lesser known peashrubs are Russian peashrub (*C. frutex*), littleleaf peashrub (*C. microphylla*), and the pygmy peashrub (*C. pygmaea*). Russian peashrub is an upright plant with a mature height of 6 feet. This species has one globe-shaped cultivar called 'Globosa' that matures at 2 to 3 feet. The littleleaf peashrub grows about 6 feet tall with a slightly wider spread. A more compact form with finer foliage is called 'Tidy.' Pygmy peashrub is a small, mounded plant with a mature height and spread of about 4 feet. It is considered by many gardening authorities to be the most attractive peashrub.

While there may be more attractive shrubs for the South Dakota landscape, it would be hard to find a tougher one. N.E. Hansen called it "one of the best, if not the very best shrub to withstand drought, cold and alkali." Peashrub has few pest problems but can be defoliated by grasshoppers and ash-gray blister beetles.

Shrubs for South Dakota

Dogwood

Tatarian dogwood	Cornus alba	Region 1-7
Pagoda dogwood	Cornus alternifolia	Region 1,2,5
Gray dogwood	Cornus racemosa	Region 1-7
Redosier dogwood	Cornus sericea	Region 1-6

Cansasa, meaning "red wood," is the Lakota name for dogwood.

Cornus alba 'Argentea-marginata'

When dogwood is mentioned in most other parts of the country, flowering dogwood (*C. florida*) comes to mind. This small, flowering tree is considered by most gardening experts to be a most attractive ornamental. Unfortunately, it is not hardy in South Dakota and would not be likely to survive the first winter.

Cornus alternifolia

The dogwoods that grace the South Dakota landscape are appreciated for their white flowers and white to bluish-black fruit. Many also have colorful foliage or twigs. The Tatarian dogwood is a tall shrub, often reaching a height of 8 feet or more with an equal spread. This dogwood has white flowers in flat-topped clusters that appear after the leaves have expanded. The flowers are followed in mid-summer by clusters of ¾-inch, white (sometimes with a bluish tint) fruit that may remain for the rest of the growing season. The twig color is red to a bright coral red, making winter the showiest season for some of the cultivars of this dogwood. One that has especially ornamental foliage is 'Argento-marginata' with creamy-white and green foliage.

Pagoda dogwood, despite the oriental sounding name, is native from the forests of Minnesota east to New Brunswick. It is also known as alternate-leaf dogwood. Pagoda dogwood may reach a height of 15 feet with a spread slightly wider than its height. This small tree is noted for its white flowers that occur in flat-topped clusters, bluish-black fruit, and reddish-purple fall color. Another striking feature of this plant is the spreading, horizontal branches that give it an "oriental" appearance.

Gray dogwood can become a large shrub, often more than 10 feet tall. This shrub also suckers profusely so its spread can be 15 feet or more. The flowers and fruit are similar to Tatarian dogwood. The color of a new stem is a light reddish brown that becomes gray as stems reach 3 years in age.

Cornus sericea

Redosier dogwood is a South Dakota native that forms thickets along many of our lakes and

streams. The Lakota mixed the powdered inner bark with tobacco and used it as a smoke. The shrub may reach a height of 10 feet with an equal spread. The flowers are white and occur in early June, but they may also appear sporadically throughout the summer. The fruit is white and ⅓ inch in diameter. The most ornamental feature of this shrub is the brightly colored young bark. The 1- and 2-year old stems can be a brilliant red. There are several common cultivars of this species. One of the best for bright red stem color is 'Cardinal.' 'Flaviramea' is a yellow-stem cultivar known as golden-twig dogwood. Two compact forms of the shrub are 'Isanti' that reaches a height of 5 to 6 feet and 'Kelseyi' that may only reach a height of 3 feet.

Dogwoods are best planted as large mass plantings due to their large mature size. The exception to this is the pagoda dogwood. This small tree can be planted as a mass or as a single specimen tree. Dogwoods perform best in a full-sun to part-sun location on a well-drained soil. They are very adaptable, however. Dogwoods can be found on sites that range from dry to moist and neutral to alkaline.

Unfortunately, dogwoods are not without problems. Pagoda dogwood may winter-kill if planted in exposed sites. Partially shaded locations protected from the winter winds are best for this plant. The other dogwoods may suffer from several stem cankers and twig blights as well as powdery mildew.

The last comment on dogwoods is that of Clarence Wedge who in a 1923 report to the South Dakota State Horticultural Society said, "The dogwoods are early bloomers, very fragrant, and some of them are loaded with pretty white or blue berries in the autumn. Bank up the house with them. Even in the shade of other trees they will do their best and ask for nothing more than a fair chance in the world."

Smokebush, Smoketree

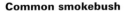

Common smokebush   *Cotinus coggygria*   Region 1,2,3,5,6

This shrub is responsible for numerous "What is that plant?" calls each summer when it comes into bloom. The small yellowish flowers form in large clusters on stalks covered with pink hairs. The overall appearance of these blooms is like a pink puff of smoke. In addition to the attractive summer blooms, the plant may also have spectacular summer and fall foliage color. 'Royal Purple' has purplish red foliage from spring to fall, and even the blooms have a purplish red color.

Common smokebush may reach a height and spread of 5 to 10 feet in South Dakota. It is not always hardy to South Dakota so it may also become a "dieback" shrub, dying to the ground over the winter only to sprout up to 4 or 5 feet during the summer growing season. Since it flowers on new wood, this should not reduce its ornamental value.

The shrub should be planted in a sunny location, but it is otherwise adaptable to sites ranging from dry to moist and neutral to alkaline.

Cotinus coggygria

Cotoneaster

Cranberry cotoneaster	*Cotoneaster apiculatus*	Region 1,2
Spreading cotoneaster	*Cotoneaster divaricatus*	Region 1,2
Hedge cotoneaster	*Cotoneaster lucidus*	Region 1-7

Cotoneaster, pronounced ko-to-nee-AS-ter, is probably one of our most common groups of shrubs in South Dakota.

Cotoneaster lucidus

The hedge cotoneaster, as the name implies, is extensively used as a hedge plant throughout the state. Its upright form and crisp foliage make it easy to shear. The flowers are not very showy, but the black, ⅖-inch fruit persists into the winter. Fall color is a mottled red and yellow and can be quite showy. Planted as a specimen and allowed to grow to its full form, it can reach a height of 10 feet or

more with a spread of 6 to 8 feet. As a hedge it can be maintained anywhere from 4 to 10 feet in height. While it is commonly seen as a hedge, it can make a stunning specimen plant and should be used more in this capacity.

Hedge cotoneaster is adaptable to a wide range of sites from dry to well-drained and neutral to alkaline pH. It can survive on moist sites but growth is often stunted. The plant does best in full sun.

Cranberry and spreading cotoneasters are smaller plants. The cranberry cotoneaster forms a dense mound with a height of 2 to 3 feet and a spread of 4 to 5 feet. Spreading cotoneaster has more of a spreading habit with a height of 5 feet and a spread of 5 to 6 feet. Interesting forms, bright red fruit, and fall color are the outstanding ornamental features of these two plants. Unfortunately they are not reliably hardy in most of the state.

Cotoneasters have a number of pest problems in South Dakota. They are susceptible to fireblight, spider mites, scales, and cotoneaster webworm, among others.

Daphne

Burkwood daphne   *Daphne x burkwoodii*   Region 1,2,5

Daphne is one of the few small, broadleaf semi-evergreens that can be planted in our state. This little-known shrub has fragrant, light pink ½-inch flowers that form in clusters similar to the herbaceous perennial plant candytuft. The berry-like red fruit is not particularly showy but the foliage is attractive. The cultivar 'Carol Mackie' has green leaves with a cream-edged margin. The foliage is usually maintained until November or December, with most of the leaves dropped by Christmas. The cultivar 'Somerset' is similar except the foliage is green. Both cultivars are excellent additions to a rock garden or other small planting.

The plant forms a very compact mound with a mature height of 2 to 3 feet and a spread of 4 to 5 feet. It performs best in full sun to light shade. The roots require cool temperatures, however, and many daphne have failed when the base of the plant is exposed to hot conditions. These shrubs should be planted in a lightly shaded site with mulch over the roots.

Daphne x burkwoodii

While mulch is necessary to keep the roots cool, the plants should not be subjected to wet soils. The soil must be well-drained. Unlike many other species of daphne, the burkwood and its cultivars are very adaptable to alkaline soils.

Daphne suffers from few pest problems in our state. Most failures can be attributed to planting on poorly suited sites. The shrub does not tolerate transplanting very well and should not be moved once established in the landscape.

Dwarf bush-honeysuckle

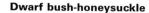

Dwarf bush-honeysuckle   *Diervilla lonicera*   Region 1,2,3,5,6

Despite the name, this mounding, spreading plant is not closely related to honeysuckle. Dwarf bush-honeysuckle has small sulfur-yellow flowers that form small clusters during the summer. The fruit is not showy but the glossy green foliage turns a reddish color in the fall.

Dwarf bush-honeysuckle is a mounding plant that reaches a height of 3 to 4 feet and a spread of 3 to 5 feet. The plant suckers profusely so it generally forms a large mass. This is an excellent plant for hillsides or other areas that need cover.

Dwarf bush-honeysuckle is a very adaptable plant tolerating a wide range of soil conditions from dry to moist and neutral to pH 7.5. The plant does best in full sun, but will also tolerate some shade.

Diervilla lonicera

Burning bush, Winged Euonymus, Winged wahoo

Burning bush	*Euonymus alatus*	Region 1-6
Eastern wahoo	*Euonymus atropurpureus*	Region 1,2,3,5,6

Fall is the season for Euonymus. Burning bush takes its name from the brilliant red fall color of its foliage. The native species, eastern wahoo, sometimes also referred to as burning bush, has excellent fall foliage color, as well as bright red seed pods during the fall. The corked or winged bark of both species also provides winter interest.

Burning bush is a rounded plant with a mature height and spread of more than 8 feet, particularly in the mild climate of southeastern South Dakota. The dwarf burning bush 'Compactus' has a similar form but a mature height and spread approximately half that of the species. Another cultivar, 'Nordine,' while having the same mature height and spread of the species, has a denser habit and more cork on the twigs.

Eastern wahoo is native to parts of eastern South Dakota. Homesteaders found this plant to be an excellent and easily obtainable shrub for their landscape. It was described as "among the finest and most showy ornamental." Eastern wahoo can reach a height of 15 feet and a spread of 10 feet or more. It becomes very open and may not set a good fruit crop every year.

Euonymus alatus

Euonymus alatus

Burning bush and eastern wahoo are both adaptable to full-sun and part-sun locations, though the best fall color typically develops under full sun. They are also adapted to a wide range of soil textures and pH. However, they will not tolerate poorly drained sites.

Burning bush can tolerate the climate in most of the state. The dwarf, however, is not as hardy and may be injured at temperatures of –25 F, particularly if these temperatures occur during November. 'Nordine,' a seed selection from Korea, is considered to be hardier than the dwarf burning bush. Eastern wahoo is hardy to most East River locations and the Black Hills.

Burning bush and eastern wahoo have few pest problems in the state. They can be infested with scales occasionally, but their most serious pest is not an insect but rabbits. These plants have been described as "rabbit candy" and they may be eaten to the ground or completely girdled during the winter.

Euonymus atropurpureus

Forsythia, Golden bells

orsythia   *Forsythia* spp.   Region 1,2

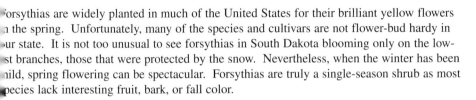

orsythias are widely planted in much of the United States for their brilliant yellow flowers n the spring. Unfortunately, many of the species and cultivars are not flower-bud hardy in ur state. It is not too unusual to see forsythias in South Dakota blooming only on the low- st branches, those that were protected by the snow. Nevertheless, when the winter has been nild, spring flowering can be spectacular. Forsythias are truly a single-season shrub as most pecies lack interesting fruit, bark, or fall color.

here are forsythias that ave been developed to e flower-bud hardy in he Dakotas. Probably he best known is 'Meadowlark,' a cross eleased by North)akota State University nd South Dakota State Jniversity that is ower-bud hardy to -35 F. Another possibil- y is 'Northern Sun,' ntroduced by the Minnesota Landscape Arboretum and flower- ud hardy to –30 F.

Forsythia spp.

hese hardy forsythias are large plants, often reaching a nature height of 8 feet with a equal spread. They all have semi-arching habit. Forsythias do best in a full-sun loca- on and in a moist well-drained soil with a neutral pH.

)ne other forsythia is occasionally planted in the land- cape. The dwarf forsythia 'Bronxensis' is a small (3 feet ll) mounding shrub as well known for its bronze fall olor as for its yellow spring flowers. It is an excellent lant for mass planting but it is not flower-bud hardy in pen winters.

Sea buckthorn, Siberian sandthorn

Sea buckthorn   *Hippophae rhamnoides*   Region 1,2,5

While this is a fairly rare shrub in the landscape, it has been planted in South Dakota for more than 100 years. This is one of the best plants for winter fruit color. The attractive ⅕-inch, orange-yellow berries remain on the plant into the winter and even into the spring. The fruit is very acidic and is not taken by many birds, but it is a favorite food of pheasants. The fruit can be made into a drink known as "poor man's orange juice." The silver-green summer foliage provides an attractive contrast to the typical green color of other shrubbery.

Sea buckthorn becomes a large and open shrub with a mature height of 10 feet and an equal spread. The plant is adapted to sandy, infertile soils and may perform poorly in heavy, fertile soils. It does best in full sun.

Sea buckthorn has few problems in the South Dakota landscape. It does sucker profusely so it can spread out into the surrounding landscape. It can be held in place with annual pruning. The plant is dioecious, so there are separate male and female plants. To ensure good fruiting, plant six females to every one male.

Hippophae rhamnoides

Hydrangea

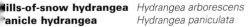
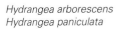

Hills-of-snow hydrangea   *Hydrangea arborescens*   Region 1,2,5
Panicle hydrangea   *Hydrangea paniculata*   Region 1,2,3,5,6

Hydrangeas are one of our best-known summer flowering plants. They begin blooming just as the blooms of spring flowering plants fade and they may continue flowering until late summer. The flowers are usually white but often have a pinkish cast as they age. Dried, the flowers are sometimes used in winter bouquets.

Hills-of-snow hydrangea, also know as snowhill hydgrangea, has two very common cultivars, 'Annabelle' and 'Grandiflora.' Annabelle becomes a rounded plant about 5 feet tall. It has large heads, often 10 inches across, of snow-white flowers. It also thrives in shade, an unusual characteristic for a flowering shrub. Grandiflora generally becomes a little taller at maturity and the flower heads are a little smaller. Grandiflora prefers full or part sun.

Panicle hydrangea has one very common cultivar also known as 'Grandiflora' or 'PeeGee' hydrangea. This old favorite has large (12- to 18-inch) clusters of white flowers. The PeeGee hydrangea becomes a tall shrub and can reach a height and spread of 8 feet. 'Compact,' a tighter form, only becomes about 6 feet tall at maturity.

Hydrangea arborescens

Hydrangea paniculata

There is one other hydrangea to mention. While it is not commonly available in South Dakota garden centers, it is a regular feature of mail-order catalogs. The 'Nikko Blue' hydrangea is noted for its ability to change flower color depending upon the soil pH. On neutral soils the flowers are pink and on acidic soils they are blue. While this is an interesting characteristic, the plant is not reliably hardy in much of our state.

Privet

Common privet   *Ligustrum vulgare*   Region 1,2

Privet is probably the most common hedge shrub in the United States. It has all the necessary characteristics of a hedge plant: small foliage, ability to sprout readily from shearing, and a dense branching pattern. The white flowers are small and not very showy. They also have what can best be described as an odor, rather than a fragrance. Shiny black fruit occurs in the fall, but they are of little ornamental value.

Ligustrum vulgare

The glossy, deep-green foliage, which often persists into the winter, is the primary ornamental value. There are several golden-leafed privets available, with the golden vicary privet, *L.* x *vicaryi*, being the most common.

Privet generally can reach a height of 4 or 5 feet. The shape is somewhat upright although the spread can often equal the height. The cultivar 'Lodense' is a more compact form usually not becoming more than 3 feet tall at maturity.

While privet has a number of fine ornamental qualities, it is not reliably hardy in our state. Hansen's reports on his 1920s trials with privet repeatedly mention that the plants winter-killed in Brookings. Privet has a tendency to continue growing late into the fall, and the tender branches often are killed if temperatures drop into the teens during October.

One of the hardiest common privets is 'Cheyenne,' a selection made in Cheyenne, Wyo. However, even this cultivar frequently dies back in severe winters. Regel privet, *L. obtusifolium* var. *regelianum* is another of the hardiest privets but may also winter-kill.

Honeysuckle

Wild honeysuckle	*Lonicera hirsuta*	Region 1-7
Sakhalin honeysuckle	*Lonicera maximowiczii* var. *sachalinensis*	Region 1-7
Tatarian honeysuckle	*Lonicera tatarica*	Region 1-7
European fly honeysuckle	*Lonicera xylosteum*	Region 1-7

Caniskuye is the Lakota name for the wild honeysuckle.

Lonicera tatarica

Flowers and fruit are two ornamental characteristics of these common ornamental shrubs. The flowers may be white, yellow, or pink depending upon the species and cultivar, but all occur in the spring after the leaves appear. These are followed by small berries which are readily taken by birds. Only the Sakhalin honeysuckle has fall color.

The most common honeysuckle in South Dakota is the Tatarian honeysuckle. This shrub may become anywhere from 6 to 15 feet tall with an equal spread. The pink to white flowers appear in June and are followed by small orange to red fruit in July and August. This plant is widely planted as a windbreak or hedge and it also frequently comes up in gardens and borders, as birds will carry the seeds everywhere. There are numerous cultivars of Tatarian honeysuckle, with most differing in flower color or resistance to the honeysuckle aphid.

Another commonly planted shrub is the European fly honeysuckle. This is a more compact plant, generally only reaching a height of 3 feet with a spread of 4 feet. The cultivar 'Emerald Mound' has yellowish-green flowers in the spring and dark red berries in the fall. A similar plant is 'Miniglobe' honeysuckle. It has form and size similar to Emerald Mound but has denser growth and is hardier. The flowers and fruit, however, are not very conspicuous.

Though not commonly planted, the Sakhalin honeysuckle is attractive. The flowers are a deep purple-red and are larger than those on the typical honeysuckle. The foliage is probably its best ornamental feature. The leaves have a reddish cast when they first appear in the spring and turn deep green during the summer and then a brilliant golden yellow in the fall. This is one of the few honeysuckles that has a good fall color. Sakhalin honeysuckle may reach a height of 10 feet with an equal spread.

There are many other honeysuckles that can be planted in South Dakota. The Amur honeysuckle, *L. maackii*, is a large shrub with horizontally spreading branches and fragrant white to yellow flowers. There is also a honeysuckle native to South Dakota, wild honeysuckle, *L. hirsuta*, which is found infrequently in the Black Hills and in scattered locations throughout the state. Vining or tumpet honeysuckle, *L. sempervirens*, is covered in the vine section of this book.

Lonicera xylosteum

Honeysuckles perform best in full-sun locations, although part sun is also acceptable. They are very tolerant of soil conditions and will do well in alkaline soils. They are better adapted to dry soils rather than wet and may fail if planted in locations that are flooded during the spring.

When Hansen wrote in 1931 that, "Tatarian honeysuckle is very free from insect attack," the honeysuckle aphid had not yet reached our country. This small sucking insect entered the U.S. from Russia sometime in the early 1980s. The infestation results in the honeysuckle terminals becoming curled and distorted, an appearance referred to as witches' broom. While the plants rarely die from the attack, they will look unsightly. Chemical control is often not practical due to the number of applications needed each year.

The best solution is to avoid planting susceptible plants. Tatarian honeysuckle is very susceptible to the honeysuckle aphid, though certain cultivars such as 'Arnold Red' often are less infested than the species. Several cultivars such as 'Freedom' and 'Honeyrose' have similar characteristics to the Tatarian honeysuckle but are fairly resistant to the aphid. The European fly and Sakhalin honeysuckles are also resistant.

Most honeysuckles are also heavily browsed by deer.

Grapeholly, Mahonia

Creeping mahonia *Mahonia repens* Region 1,2,5

The name grape holly is an excellent description of this low-growing plant. The evergreen, bluish-green foliage closely resembles holly leaves. Blue-black berries form in grape-like clusters during early summer and can be used in jellies. In addition to these outstanding ornamental qualities, the foliage also develops a purplish-bronze cast in the fall, and the plant is covered with yellow flowers in the spring.

Mahonia repens

Creeping mahonia is a groundcover that reaches a height of 1 or 2 feet but may spread to several times its height. There is also a taller mahonia, the Oregon grapeholly, *M. aquifolium*, that is not hardy in South Dakota.

Creeping mahonia is native to the Black Hills and can be readily found beneath ponderosa pines. The plant does best in a full-sun or part-sun location but does need some protection from winter sun. Well-drained, slightly acidic soils are ideal; however, it will tolerate slightly alkaline soils as well.

This plant's primary problem is the South Dakota winter. It may winter-kill if it is not covered with snow. It may also severely winter-burn in open winters. The best winter protection is to cover the plant with evergreen branches during the winter or plant it in a location with reliable snow cover.

Mockorange

 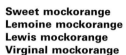

Sweet mockorange	*Philadelphus coronarius*	Region 1-6
Lemoine mockorange	*Philadelphus x lemoinei*	Region 1,2,5
Lewis mockorange	*Philadelphus lewisii*	Region 1,2,5
Virginal mockorange	*Philadelphus x virginalis*	Region 1,2,3,5

Hansen stated it best when he wrote, "the mockorange is unsurpassed for the delicious and intense fragrance of the flowers." The white blossoms of the mockorange produce a heavy, sweet, orange-like fragrance in late spring. This is its only ornamental value, however, as the woody fruit is insignificant and there is no fall color.

Philadelphus coronarius

Sweet mockorange can reach a height of 10 feet with an equal spread. While this was once the most commonly planted mockorange, it has been surpassed by many newer cultivars. There is still one cultivar of sweet mockorange frequently planted, the golden mockorange, 'Aureus.' It is usually only half the mature height and spread of the species. Its ornamental value is the golden foliage during the summer and fall. However, in the hot, dry August weather the golden leaves may brown at the margin.

The Lemoine mockorange is not commonly sold in South Dakota but may be seen in gardening catalogs. There are several cultivars such as 'Avalanche' and 'Mont Blanc' that have attractive and fragrant flowers, but these plants may suffer tip dieback during the winter unless planted in a sheltered location.

Lewis mockorange is the state flower of Idaho. There is one outstanding cultivar, 'Blizzard,' which has white, fragrant flowers. Its floral display may last up to 4 weeks, much longer than the typical mockorange. It is also a very hardy plant. The cultivar has an upright form, with a mature height and spread of 5 and 4 feet, respectively.

The virginal mockorange reaches a height of 6 to 8 feet with a spread of 5 to 6 feet. One of the best known cultivars is 'Minnesota Snowflake' with fragrant double white flowers.

Philadelphus coronarius 'Aureus'

There are also a number of cultivars that originated from crosses. 'Miniature Snowflake' is a dwarf, compact plant with a mature height of 2 or 3 feet and a spread of 2 feet. It has very fragrant, double white flowers.

Mockoranges do best in a full-sun location, preferably with some winter protection. They do not have demanding soil requirements and will tolerate a wide range of soil moisture and pH up to 7.5. They also have few serious pest problems. The most common problem is browning foliage during hot, dry weather.

Ninebark

| **Mountain ninebark** | *Physocarpus monogynus* | Region 1-6 |
| **Common ninebark** | *Physocarpus opulifolius* | Region 1-7 |

Ninebarks are rarely planted in the landscape, a fate common to many native species. On the surface, ninebarks appear to have little to recommend them over other shrubs. However, the peeling bark and reddish seed pods provide some winter interest. Many of the cultivars also have a neat, compact shape, and several have colorful foliage.

Mountain ninebark has a height and spread of about 3 feet. The shape is compact and it can make an attractive hedge plant. It is native to the Black Hills. It has round clusters of white spiraea-like flowers in spring and again in late summer.

Common ninebark can become a large shrub, often 10 feet tall with an equal spread. Generally cultivars are planted rather than the species. Each of three commonly planted cultivars has its own unique ornamental value. 'Nugget' ninebark, a South Dakota State University introduction, becomes about 6 feet tall with a spread of 5 feet. Spring foliage starts out as a golden-yellow and becomes lime green by summer. 'Dart's Gold' is slightly smaller at maturity and has a yellow foliage color. 'Snowfall' is one of the few ninebarks selected for its large, white flowers which appear in May or June. This cultivar is the largest of the three, often reaching a height of 7 or 8 feet.

Physocarpus monogynus

Ninebarks do best in a full-sun location, but they will tolerate light shade. They are not very demanding about soil conditions and can be found on a wide variety of sites. Powdery mildew can become a problem in shaded sites.

Physocarpus opulifolius

Potentilla, Shrubby cinquefoil

Potentilla   *Potentilla fruticosa*   Region 1-7

If green ash is the most common tree in the South Dakota landscape, then potentilla is one of the most common shrubs. The bright yellow flowers that appear throughout late spring to summer are probably the reason for its popularity. Yet while yellow is the most common color, there also are white and pink flowering cultivars. There is also a wide range in summer foliage color from dark green to silver-gray. Most cultivars do not have a fall color, and in all, the fruit is insignificant.

Because of the popularity of this particular plant and the wide range of growing conditions, it is easier to list cultivars rather than merely name them. The following list is an example of the range of ornamental features for this attractive group of plants.

Potentilla fruticosa 'Abbotswood'

Cultivar	Flower color	Foliage color	Height
'Abbotswood'	white	blue-green	3 feet
'Absaraka'[1]	deep yellow	deep blue-green	3 feet
'Coronation Triumph'	yellow	gray-green	4 feet
'Fargo'[2]	golden yellow	bright green	3 feet
'Goldfinger'	golden yellow	dark green	3 feet
'Jackmannii'	deep yellow	dark green	3 feet
'Katherine Dykes'	lemon yellow	silver-green	3 feet
'Longacre'	sulfur-yellow	shiny dark green	2 feet
'McKay's White'	white	light green	3 feet
'Pink Beauty'	pink	green	3 feet
'Primerose Beauty'	pale yellow	silver-gray	3 feet
'Snowbird'	double white	glossy green	3 feet

[1] sold as Dakota Goldrush®
[2] sold as Dakota Sunspot®

Potentilla fruticosa 'Jackmannii'

Potentillas do best in full sun. If planted in shade, they often become very open and the blooms are sparse. Many are tolerant of alkaline or dry soils. They do not perform well in wet soils.

Potentillas have few pest problems. Some will become chlorotic on alkaline soils. Most can become infested with spider mites if allowed to grow too dense or if planted in a hot, dry location. Potentillas often require annual renewal pruning to look their best.

Potentilla fruticosa 'McKay's White'

Purpleleaf sand cherry

Purpleleaf sand cherry   *Prunus* x *cistena*   Region 1-6

Cistena is the Lakota word for "baby."

This plant is an introduction by N.E. Hansen and is described in numerous garden books as "the shrub from South Dakota" (and occasionally North Dakota, as many people seem to

confuse the two states). G.B. Tuthill, an avid Sioux Falls gardener, described this plant best in a 1931 letter to the South Dakota Horticulture Society. *"Prunus cistena* is the most unique and outstanding of all shrubs introduced by Prof. N.E. Hansen of South Dakota State College. The glossy brilliant purplish red foliage, showy wine colored blossoms and fruit, and low compact habit of growth, together with absolute hardiness makes this the finest and most dependable of all low growing red or purple leaf shrubs. Its rich color tones are invaluable for landscape and foundation plantings."

Cistena, the Lakota word for "baby," is a good name for a plant that reaches a mature height of only 6 to 8 feet with a spread of 5 to 6 feet. As with all cherries, it should be planted in a full-sun location on a well-drained soil. Soils that remain wet for several days may be fatal to this plant.

Purpleleaf sand cherry has few serious pest problems, but it can be partially defoliated by pear slugs.

Buckthorn

Rhamnus cathartica

Rhamnus frangula

are flowers yellowish-green

Common buckthorn	*Rhamnus cathartica*	Region 1-7
Glossy buckthorn	*Rhamnus frangula*	Region 1,2,3,5

Buckthorn, particularly common buckthorn, has become too prevalent in the South Dakota landscape. While the plant is native to Europe and Asia, it has spread to every forest and windbreak in eastern South Dakota. The small, black fruit is readily taken by birds; thus, the seeds are deposited across the landscape.

Rhamnus cathartica

Common buckthorn can become a small tree, crowding out more desirable vegetation. It occasionally is confused for a crabapple because of its form, or a chokecherry because of its black fruit, but buckthorn has none of their ornamental characteristics. If people remark they have a crabapple that never flowers but produces an abundance of small berries that stain the walkways, they probably have a common buckthorn. The plant also serves as an alternate host for crown rust of oats. There is no reason to plant a shrub that is more nuisance than asset to the ornamental landscape.

The same can not be said of the glossy buckthorn. While it is sometimes an alternate host to oat rust, this species is not invasive. It is an excellent ornamental plant with several

Rhamnus frangula 'Tallcole'

Rhamnus frangula 'Asplenifolia'

outstanding cultivars. 'Tallcole,' also known as 'Tallhedge®,' is a narrow, upright shrub that may reach 15 feet or more yet maintain a spread of only 3 or 4 feet. The foliage is a dark glossy green that turns a yellowish-green to golden yellow in the fall. The branching pattern is so dense that even in winter it provides a screen.

The second cultivar is 'Asplenifolia,' otherwise known as the fernleaf buckthorn. This plant has very unusual cut leaves that appear almost fernlike. Fernleaf buckthorn can become an upright shrub about 12 feet tall with a spread of 8 feet.

Buckthorns do best in well-drained soil in a full-sun location. They will tolerate shade, as witnessed by the number of common buckthorns growing in any shelterbelt.

Azalea, Rhododendron

 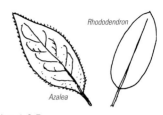

Azalea	*Rhododendron* spp.	Region 1,2,5
Rhododendron	*Rhododendron* spp.	Region 1,2

"The cultivated rhododendrons of eastern nurseries are conspicuous by their absence from northwestern catalogs, owning to entire lack of hardiness," wrote Hansen in 1901. Fortunately, there are now azaleas and rhododendrons that can be planted in our state so we can enjoy some of the same beauty that graces the gardens of New England, the South, and the Pacific Northwest.

Azaleas and rhododendron are in the same genus, *Rhododendron*, but they are different plants. While the differences are primarily in the flower parts, the major distinction made by most northern gardeners is that azaleas are deciduous (they drop their leaves in the fall) while rhododendrons are evergreen.

There are a number of azaleas that have been developed by the University of Minnesota to withstand winter temperatures as low as -35 F to -45 F without injury to the plant or flower buds. These hardy plants are referred to as the Lights series and all bear the word Lights as part of their name. The following are some of the Lights series available to South Dakota gardeners.

Cultivar	Flower color	Foliage color	Fall color	Height
'Golden Lights'	golden	dark green	bronzy-red	4 feet
'Mandarin Lights'	orange	green	none	4 feet
'Northern Lights'	pink	deep green	none	4 feet
'Orchid Lights'	lilac	green	none	3 feet
'Rosy Lights'	rosy pink	green	none	4 feet
'Spicy Lights'	apricot-orange	deep green	none	4 feet
'White Lights'	white	dark green	bronzy-purple	5 feet

While the effort to develop hardy rhododendrons has not been as extensive as for azaleas, there are still a number of possibilities for South Dakota gardeners. The two most common are the 'P.J.M.' and 'Northern Starburst' rhododendrons. The P.J.M. rhododendron is one of the hardiest evergreen rhododendrons. The flowers are lavender and occur on the tips of branches covered with glossy green foliage. This same foliage turns a rich mahogany in the fall. The P.J.M. rhododendron reaches a height of 4 or 5 feet.

The cultivar Northern Sunburst is an improvement on the P.J.M. The large flowers are a rich pink. The leaves are a glossy green, turning purplish-brown in the fall. This plant can become 4 or 5 feet tall.

Rhododendron 'P.J.M'

While there are azaleas and rhododendrons that are hardy in our low winter temperatures, this is not the only barrier to their use in South Dakota. In addition to low mid-winter temperatures, we also experience wide temperature fluctuations in the fall and spring. An early or late freeze may injure the flower buds. The evergreen rhododendrons must also be protected from the winter sun.

Soils also prove to be a challenge to growing these plants. Azaleas and rhododendrons require a slightly acidic, well-drained sandy peat soil to perform at their best. While it is possible to grow them on an alkaline, clay soil, the chances of success are much reduced.

Sumac

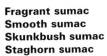

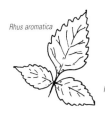

Rhus aromatica

Rhus typhina

Fragrant sumac	*Rhus aromatica*	Region 1,2,3,5,6
Smooth sumac	*Rhus glabra*	Region 1-7
Skunkbush sumac	*Rhus trilobata*	Region 1-7
Staghorn sumac	*Rhus typhina*	Region 1-7

Fragrant sumac is called *canunkcemna*, "a bad smell," while smooth sumac is *canzi*, "yellow wood," in Lakota.

Sumacs are native plants that herald the coming of fall. The bright red, orange, or scarlet fall foliage and the red clusters of fuzzy fruit heads means that winter is soon to come. Hansen called smooth sumac in fall "one of the autumnal glories of the prairie landscape."

Fragrant sumac produces small, pale yellow flowers in the spring, followed by reddish fruit. The fall color of the foliage is a brilliant scarlet to orange. The species can reach a height of 5 to 6 feet with a slightly wider spread, but there is a cultivar called 'Gro-low' that only becomes 2 to 3 feet high. This is an excellent plant for mass or hillside plantings.

Smooth sumac is also an excellent choice for mass plantings or screening. It can reach a height of 10 feet with an equal spread. The bright red fall foliage color and the scarlet seed heads are very attractive. The plant does spread, however, so it should be planted in an area where this will not become a problem.

Rhus aromatica

Rhus typhina

Skunkbush sumac is similar to fragrant sumac except for its slightly taller mature size, 6 feet, and a more upright form. The leaves and flowers are also slightly smaller. The skunkbush is very tolerant of dry soils.

Staghorn sumac received the name staghorn because of the dense velvety hairs that cover the stout branches. The plant, as with all sumacs, is best known for its fall foliage and fruit color. Staghorn sumac can reach a height of 10 feet or more with a spread of 15 feet. It also will profusely sucker. There is a cutleaf cultivar known as 'Laciniata' that has a more fernlike appearance.

Sumacs do best in full sun. They are not demanding in their soil requirements.

Poison ivy (*Toxicodendron radicans*) was formerly placed in the same genus as sumac. While sumacs are not poisonous, their sap may irritate the skin of some people.

Currant

Ribes alpinum

Ribes odoratum

Alpine currant	*Ribes alpinum*	Region 1-6
Buffalo or clove currant	*Ribes odoratum*	Region 1-7

Wica gnaskahu is Lakota for buffalo currant.

Currants are probably better known for their fruit than their appearance, but there are a few that find their place in the residential landscape. Perhaps the best known ornamental is the alpine current. This is an excellent hedge plant due to its dense growth, ability to respond to shearing, and small foliage. The small scarlet fruit is also attractive but is rarely seen in the landscape as the male plants are usually available for sale. Male currants are less apt to serve as alternate hosts to white pine blister rust. The plant is about 3 to 5 feet tall at maturity with a slightly wider spread. There is a slightly smaller cultivar available known as 'Green Mound' alpine currant.

The buffalo or clove currant is a South Dakota native and deserves more attention than it receives. The plant is covered with fragrant yellow flowers in the spring. These are followed by clusters of small black berries that can be used in jellies. Buffalo currant can become a rather large shrub, almost 10 feet tall with an equal spread.

Currants are adaptable to either a sunny or shady location. They are also tolerant of heavy clay soils with a pH up to 7.5. Spider mites and powdery mildew can sometimes become a problem.

Ribes alpinum

Bristly locust, Roseacacia locust, Rose-acacia

Rose-acacia   *Robinia hispida*   Region 1-6

Rose-acacia is rarely found in garden centers anymore but can often be seen in the gardens of older homes. The most attractive attribute of this plant is its long clusters of rose-col-

ored, pea-like flowers in mid-summer. The flowers, while extremely showy, are not fragrant. The fruit is a small brown-black pod but is rarely produced. The pinnately compound foliage is a light green during the summer and changes to a yellow green in the fall. Rose-acacia can reach a height of 6 to 8 feet with an equal spread. It suckers profusely so it will sometimes form a mass planting.

Rose-acacia is adapted to poor soils and is used to stabilize banks in some parts of the eastern U.S. It has few serious pest problems but may experience dieback during severe winters. It should be annually pruned.

Robinia hispida

Dwarf Arctic blue willow

Dwarf Arctic blue willow   *Salix purpurea* 'Nana'   Region 1,2,3,5

While willows are often medium to large trees, this particular cultivar stays fairly compact. At maturity the plant is about 5 feet tall with an equal or slightly wider spread. Dwarf Arctic blue willow has narrow, bluish-green foliage and slender purplish twigs. The plant responds well to shearing and makes an attractive hedge.

Dwarf Arctic blue willow is best planted in a full-sun location. Soil pH is not critical but dry soils should be avoided. There are few serious pest problems.

Salix purpurea 'Nana'

Elder, Elderberry

American elderberry	*Sambucus canadensis*	Region 1-7
Scarlet elder	*Sambucus pubens*	Region 1-7
European red elder	*Sambucus racemosa*	Region 1-7

Chaputa is Lakota for elderberry. The berries were eaten fresh or used to make a drink.

Elderberries are seldom seen in the South Dakota ornamental landscape but they do offer some interesting possibilities. Elderberries are covered with clusters of fragrant white flowers in the spring. In mid-summer, clusters of purplish-black to red fruit are readily taken by birds. If you can beat the birds to the berries, they make excellent wine and jellies.

American elderberry can become a large plant, often reaching a height and spread of 10 feet. American elderberry has clusters of white flowers in the spring and blue to black berries in mid-summer. The fruit can be used in pies, jellies, and wine. Two cultivars selected for their fruit are 'Adams' and 'York.' Better fruit set will occur if one of each cultivar is planted. There is also a cultivar called 'Aurea,' the golden elder, that has golden yellow leaves during the summer. However, these leaves may brown in hot, dry weather.

The scarlet elder is about the same size as the American. The primary difference between the two is that scarlet elder has red fruit in the summer. It is also one of the first plants to leaf out in the spring and flowers earlier than the American elderberry. The European red elder is similar to the scarlet elder. It is not commonly used in the landscape except for its golden-leafed cultivar 'Sutherland Golden.'

Sambucus canadensis

Elderberries can grow in full-sun to shady locations. They are generally found along rivers and streams and do better on moist soils than dry ones. They have few pest problems.

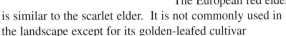

Buffaloberry

Silver buffaloberry *Shepherdia argentea* Region 1-7

Mastinca pute can is Lakota for buffaloberry. The fruit was dried for winter use.

The silver buffaloberry takes its common name from the silvery-gray foliage. Flowers are small and yellow and are not very showy. The fruit, however, is very ornamental.

The orange-red ⅙-inch fruits remain on the shrub through the summer. They are edible and are quickly eaten by wildlife. The berries make excellent jelly and can be usually harvested after the first frost by shaking the branches and catching the berries on a tarp. Silver buffaloberry has separate male and female plants, so both must be planted if fruit is desired.

Silver buffaloberry is a native shrub that can become tree-like. The plant can reach 12 feet or more at maturity with a similar spread. The plant has thorns so can be used as a barrier.

Shepherdia argentea

Silver buffaloberry prefers sunny locations; otherwise, it can be planted almost anywhere except on extremely wet soils. It has very few pest problems.

leaf spirea, Falsespirea, Ural falsespirea

Ural falsespirea   *Sorbaria sorbifolia*   Region 1-6

This is an old favorite that is regaining popularity. The most outstanding ornamental feature of this plant are the large (4- to 8-inches across) clusters of creamy white flowers that cover the shrub in mid-summer. Leaves have a reddish tinge when they are first expanding and then remain green until fall. The foliage is composed of small leaflets, giving the plant a fernlike appearance.

Sorbaria sorbifolia

Ural falsespirea may reach a height of 6 feet or more and will have a spread often wider than its height. It suckers profusely so it will form a mass rather than remain an individual shrub.

The plant is adaptable and can thrive on sites that range from full sun to light shade. It is also very tolerant of a wide range of soil pH up to 7.5. It does better on moist soils than dry. Ural falsespirea has few serious pest problems.

Spirea

Japanese white spirea	*Spiraea albiflora*	Region 1,2,3,5
Garland spirea	*Spiraea* x *arguta*	Region 1,2,5
Bumalda spirea	*Spiraea* x *bumalda*	Region 1-6
Japanese spirea	*Spiraea japonica*	Region 1,2
Nippon spirea	*Spiraea nipponica*	Region 1,2,5
Bridalwreath spirea	*Spiraea prunifolia*	Region 1,2,5
Threelobe spirea	*Spiraea trilobata*	Region 1,2,3,5
Vanhoutte spirea	*Spiraea* x *vanhouttei*	Region 1,2,3,5,6

As the length of the above list implies, spireas are the shrub for South Dakota. While they are often overused in the residential landscape, they also are very adaptable to our climate and soils.

Spiraea x bumalda

Their ornamental values are numerous. Many spireas, and particularly the cultivars, are low- to medium-sized plants that will not overgrow their location. Many spireas also have interesting foliage, either in summer color or shape. The flowers, occurring in rounded or flat clusters, are very attractive and occur either in spring or summer depending upon the species. While spireas should not be overplanted, it is also hard to find a landscape where they will not be an asset.

Spireas vary widely in their flower color and season, their foliage, and their mature height. Due to the large number of species and cultivars available in garden centers across the state, it is easier to list them than provide a description of each.

CULTIVAR	FLOWER color; season	FOLIAGE summer; fall	HEIGHT
Japanese white spirea	white, summer	green; none	2 feet

| *Garland spirea* | | | |
| 'Compacta'[1] | white, spring | green; none | 4 feet |

Bumalda spirea			
'Anthony Waterer'	rose-pink, summer	reddish-purple/green; reddish	3 feet
'Coccinea'[2]	crimson, summer	bluish-green; none	3 feet
'Crispa'	pink, summer	reddish and twisted; none	3 feet
'Dart's Red'	red, summer	bluish-green; reddish-purple	3 feet
'Goldflame'	crimson, summer	mottled copper; red and orange	3 feet

Japanese spirea			
'Alpina'[3]	pink, summer	blue green; none	1 foot
'Mertyann'[4]	pink, summer	yellowish gold; pinkish-red	1 foot
'Little Princess'	pink, summer	light green; reddish	2 feet
'Magic Carpet'	deep pink, summer	light green; reddish	2 feet

Nippon spirea			
'Halward's Silver'	white, spring	dark green; none	3 feet
'Snowmound'	white, spring	dark green; none	4 feet

| *Bridalwreath spirea* | white, spring | blue green; none | 6 feet |

CULTIVAR	FLOWER color; season	FOLIAGE summer; fall	HEIGHT
Threelobe spirea 'Fairy Queen'	white, spring	dark green; none	3 feet
Vanhoutte spirea 'Renaissance'	white, spring	bluish green; none	6 feet
Additional spireas 'Goldmound' spirea 'Grefsheim' spirea	pink, summer white, spring	light yellow; pinkish red sea green; none	2 feet 5 feet

[1] sold as the Dwarf Garland spirea®
[2] sold as the Dwarf Red Flowering spirea
[3] sold as the Daphne spirea
[4] sold as the Dakota Goldcharm spirea®

Spiraea nipponica

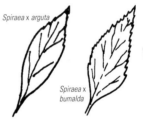

Spiraea x arguta

Spiraea x bumalda

Spiraea x vanhouttei

Spiraea prunifolia

Spiraea japonica 'Little Princess'

Spireas perform best in full-sun locations, but they will tolerate part sun though the flowers may be less abundant. They will grow in a wide range of soils except on wet sites. Most spireas, with the exception of Japanese white spirea, dwarf garland spirea, and the Daphne spirea, are tolerant of alkaline soils.

Spireas do have a number of pest problems, though none are serious enough to kill the plant. Leaf rollers, small insects that cause the leaf to curl, and a leaf spot disease are the most common problems in South Dakota. Rabbits can also eat the plants to the ground. However, this can almost be considered a plus as spireas require annual pruning to look their best. Time of pruning depends on when the plant flowers. Spring flowering spireas should be pruned after they flower. Summer flowering spireas should be pruned in late winter.

Spiraea nipponica 'Snowmound'

Coralberry, Snowberry, Wolfberry

Symphoricarpos albus

Symphoricarpos orbiculatus

White snowberry	*Symphoricarpos albus*	Region 1-7
Chenault coralberry	*Symphoricarpos* x *chenaultii*	Region 1
Wolfberry	*Symphoricarpos occidentalis*	Region 1-7
Coralberry	*Symphoricarpos orbiculatus*	Region 1-7

Wolfberry is *on sunk nasapi,* "stem to hunt dogs with" in Lakota.

The snowberries are probably one of our most overlooked groups of plants. True, they do not provide the floral display of many other ornamentals, nor is there any significant fall color. They do, however, have attractive fall and winter fruit as well as fine branches that adapt to shearing.

White snowberry reaches a height and spread of about 5 feet. The summer flowers are small and insignificant, but the large white berries that form in the fall provide interest until it snows. The summer foliage is an attractive bluish-green. The variety 'Laevigatus' is usually the one sold in garden centers as it has larger fruit than the species.

Symphoricarpos albus

The Chenault coralberry is generally available as the cultivar 'Hancock.' The plant is a low, spreading shrub with a mature height of 3 feet and a spread of more than 6 feet. As with the white snowberry, the flowers are insignificant, but the rose-pink berries add much fall interest. The side of the fruit closest to the sun turns the brightest pink. The summer foliage is a dark blue-green.

Wolfberry is not generally available in garden centers but can be found in woodlands across the state. It has a mature height and spread of 3 to 4 feet. The fruit is brown and not as attractive as the other snowberries, but wolfberry is one of the "deer-proof" plants. It spreads by rhizomes, sometimes becoming hard to contain.

Symphoricarpos orbiculatis

Coralberry, or red snowberry, is a medium-sized spreading shrub. It has a mature height of 4 or 5 feet and a spread of 5 to 8 feet. The purplish-red berries remain on the plant through the winter and contrast nicely against snow, unlike white snowberry. The summer foliage is blue-green.

Snowberries are adaptable to full-sun to shade locations. In fact, their ability to grow in shade is one of their ornamental values. They do sucker profusely so they should be planted in an area where expansion will not cause problems.

Snowberries can tolerate a wide range of soil conditions. There is only one serious problem that can ruin the ornamental value of the plant: An anthracnose disease infects the fruits, causing them to turn brown. The disease is most common on the white snowberry.

Lilac

Syringa x chinensis

Syringa villosa

Syringa vulgaris

Chinese lilac	Syringa x chinensis	Region 1,2,3,5
Hyacinth lilac	Syringa x hyacinthiflora	Region 1,2,3,5,6
Meyer lilac	Syringa meyeri	Region 1-7
Littleleaf lilac	Syringa microphylla	Region 1,2,3,5
Manchurian lilac	Syringa patula	Region 1-7
Preston lilac	Syringa x prestoniae	Region 1-7
Late lilac	Syringa villosa	Region 1-7
Common lilac	Syringa vulgaris	Region 1-7

What would a landscape be without a lilac? For many, a favorite childhood memory is bringing a handful of lilac flowers home as a present to mom. The fragrance of the blooms, when placed in a vase, filled the room.

Syringa microphylla

Lilacs are known for their flowers, though a few plants have additional ornamental features. The late spring flowers range across the color chart from white, purple, blue, and even red to yellow.

However, these same attractive and often fragrant flowers sometimes result in the spring gardener devoting too much of the landscape to lilacs. Once summer arrives there is little ornamental interest to recommend lilacs. The same is true for most lilacs in fall and winter. While every landscape probably deserves a lilac or two, or perhaps even a row, there should be room for other plants as well.

Because of the many lilacs available, the following list covers only a fraction of cultivars that a gardener may find in a nursery or gardening catalog. The list does not identify all the differences among the various species. Chinese lilac has the benefit of not being a suckering plant so it will not spread out from its original location. Hyacinth lilac is an early-bloomer, usually flowering a week or two before the common lilac. It may also develop a reddish-purple fall color, though no fall color is also a possibility. The hyacinth lilac is also an extremely hardy plant. The Meyer lilac is known to flower at a very early age, often starting

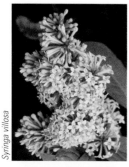

Syringa villosa

Syringa vulgaris

to bloom when it is only a foot or two tall. Littleleaf lilac has very small leaves and becomes a wide shrub, often twice as wide as tall, the plant may also have a second bloom, though only scattered through the plant, in late summer. The Manchurian lilac is one of the few lilacs to have a fall color. The Preston lilac flowers a week or two later than the common lilac, and the flowers lack the usual vibrant lilac fragrance. The late lilac is seldom planted but has characteristics similar to the Preston lilac. Common lilac can have either single or double blossoms.

Double flowering means that the number of petals have been increased. The double flowering common lilacs are French hybrids. These are the improved common lilacs that the French started developing more than a century ago. In addition to showy flowers that are either single or double, French hybrids also sucker less than the common lilac.

Syringa patula

Shrubs for South Dakota

CULTIVAR	FLOWER color; season	FOLIAGE summer; fall	HEIGHT
Chinese lilac			
'Saugeana'	lilac-red, single	green; none	10 feet
Hyacinth lilac			
'Blanche Sweet'	whitish-blue, single	green; reddish-purple or none	8 feet
'Ecel'	lilac, single	green; reddish-purple or none	10 feet
'Mount Baker'	white, single	green; reddish-purple or none	10 feet
Meyer lilac			
'Palibin'[1]	pale lilac, single	dark green; none	5 feet
Littleleaf lilac			
'Superba'	deep pink, single	green; none	6 feet
Manchurian lilac			
'Miss Kim'	pale lilac, single	green; burgundy red	6 feet
Preston lilac			
'Donald Wyman'	reddish-purple, single	dark green; none	10 feet
'James Macfarlane'	pink, single	green; none	8 feet
Late lilac	rosy to white	green; none	10 feet
Common lilac	purple, single	green; none	12 feet
'Charles Joly'	magenta, double	green; none	10 feet
'Katherine Havemeyer'	pink, double	green; none	10 feet
'Miss Ellen Willimott'	white, double	green; none	10 feet
'Mme. Lemoine'	white, double	green; none	10 feet
'Monge'	purple, single	green; none	10 feet
'President Grevy'	blue, double	green; none	10 feet
'Primrose'	light yellow, single	green; none	10 feet
Additional lilacs			
'Minuet'	lavender, single	dark green; none	8 feet
'Miss Canada'	bright pink, single	green; none	8 feet

[1] sold as Dwarf Korean lilac

All lilacs perform best in a full-sun location and a neutral, well-drained soil, tolerating an alkaline soil as long as it is not wet. Lilacs, particularly the common lilac, do suffer from a number of pest problems including borers, scales, and powdery mildew, but the biggest problem is neglect. As E.G. Sanderson wrote in a 1904 report to the South Dakota State Horticultural Society; "the scarcity and inferiority of the blossoms (is due to) the simple reason that perhaps nine-tenths of the total number are set in thick sod and never given a thought or care thereafter. Everyone set out a few, cultivate and mulch them, and note the results; there will be magnificent flowers and in abundance."

Tamarisk or Tamarix

Five-stamen tamarisk   *Tamarix ramosissima*   Region 1-7

Tamarisk is often confused by name with tamarack. Tamarack is a conifer tree that sheds its needles in the fall. Tamarisk is a shrub with fine, deciduous, scale-like leaves that somewhat resemble juniper foliage. Tamarisk's primary ornamental value is the small clusters of pink blossoms on the branch tips in July. The flowers may last up to a month. The fine-textured, almost feathery foliage also provides interest to the landscape.

Tamarisk becomes a large shrub, generally 10 feet in height and spread. It may become very open if attention is not paid to proper pruning. There are two cultivars available in garden centers. 'Cheyenne Red' has deep red flowers, while 'Summer Glow' has rosy flower spikes

Tamarisk does best in full-sun locations. It is adaptable to a wide range of pH levels, but does better on slightly acid soils. The plant is extremely hardy and is also salt tolerant.

The major difficulty in growing tamarisk is the need for proper pruning, a concern addressed by Hansen almost a century ago. At that time he wrote, "the shrub should be pruned severely every spring to give an abundance of young shoots which constitute its chief beauty." Since the flowers also occur on new wood, rejuvenation pruning will improve this as well. The plant might be better treated as a herbaceous perennial.

Tamarix ramosissima

Viburnum

 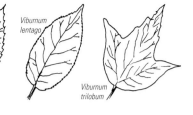

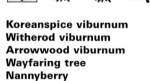

Koreanspice viburnum	*Viburnum carlesii*	Region 1
Witherod viburnum	*Viburnum cassinoides*	Region 1,2,3,5,6
Arrowwood viburnum	*Viburnum dentatum*	Region 1,2,3,5,6
Wayfaring tree	*Viburnum lantana*	Region 1,2,3,5,6
Nannyberry	*Viburnum lentago*	Region 1,2,3,5,6
European cranberrybush	*Viburnum opulus*	Region 1-6
Downy arrowwood	*Viburnum rafinesquianum*	Region 1,2,3,5,6
Sargent viburnum	*Viburnum sargentii*	Region 1,2,3,5,6
American cranberrybush	*Viburnum trilobum*	Region 1-7

Mna is the Lakota name for nannyberry.

Donald Wyman, America's preeminent gardening expert and former director of the Arnold Arboretum, once said, "A garden is not complete without a viburnum." Michael Dirr, another gardening authority and author of the *Manual of Woody Landscape Plants,* writes, "A garden without a viburnum is akin to life without music or art." Every South Dakota garden deserves a viburnum.

Viburnums are among our most versatile ornamental plants and there is at least one that will add grace to any residential landscape. This group has attractive and sometimes fragrant white spring flowers, interesting summer and fall fruit that is readily taken by wildlife (and sometimes people), and some have a brilliant red fall color, giving truly three seasons of interest.

Koreanspice viburnum is one of the most attractive and fragrant of the viburnums. The semi-snowball clusters of white flowers have an outstanding fragrance. The fall fruit is red turning to black, and the foliage may remain green or turn a wine-red. Koreanspice may achieve a height of 5 feet or more with an equal spread. Unfortunately, the plant is not reliably hardy in most of the state.

The witherod viburnum is an attractive shrub in all seasons. Expanding leaves have a purplish tint, then turn dark green. In the fall they change from orange-red to purple. The flowers are creamy white and occur in flat-topped clusters. The fall fruit starts out as pink and turns to red, then blue, then finally black. The plant may become about 5 feet tall with an equal spread.

If Koreanspice is one of the most delicate, arrowwood viburnum is one of the toughest viburnums. It tolerates

Viburnum lantana

alkaline and heavy clay soils as well as seasonal temperature fluctuations. The white flowers occur in flat clusters and the fall fruit is bright blue to blue-black. The fruit is sometimes taken so quickly by the birds that we do not have time to enjoy its appearance in the landscape. The fall color ranges from a yellow to a reddish-purple. A cultivar with consistent burgundy fall color is 'Morton,' sold as Northern Burgundy arrowwood. This cultivar and the species have a mature height of 8 to 12 feet with an equal spread. The downy arrowwood has similar characteristics but has a mature height and spread of only 6 or 7 feet.

The wayfaringtree is among the largest viburnums, sometimes reaching a height and spread of 15 feet. The large, leathery leaves are dark green in summer and turn a purplish-red in the fall; however, coloration is not consistent. The plant produces an

abundance of white flowers in the spring, though they do not have a fragrance. The fruit is probably the most outstanding feature of the plant. The ⅓-inch fruit starts in summer as yellow, then turns red, and finally black by fall. The fruit is readily taken by wildlife. There is one widely sold cultivar called 'Mohican.' This is a more compact shrub, usually only reaching a height and spread of 6 feet.

Nannyberry, also known as sheepberry, is also one of the largest viburnums, sometimes achieving a height of 20 feet, though the spread may be only 10 feet. The leaves are glossy green and may develop a reddish tinge in the fall. The flowers are white and occur in flat-topped clusters. They have a pleasant fragrance. The fruit, as with the wayfaringtree, is probably its most outstanding ornamental feature. The ½-inch fruit starts out as green, then turns yellow, pink, and finally bluish-black. The fruit is quickly taken by the birds, but if you can beat them, you'll find the fruit sweet and delicious.

Nannyberry is native along Big Stone Lake, the Big Sioux River, and in the Black Hills.

European cranberrybush is not a true cranberry, but the fruit is its best ornamental feature. The ¼-inch fruit turns a bright red in the fall and often remains on the plant through the entire winter, only to be taken by the birds as they arrive back in the spring. The flowers are white and occur in flat-topped clusters. Fall color can range from green to a reddish-purple. European cranberrybush can reach a height of 10 feet with an equal spread. There are two well-known cultivars. 'Nanum,' the dwarf European cranberrybush, is a small, compact plant that usually does not become any larger than 2 or 3 feet. It rarely produces flowers or fruit, nor is there any fall color. The common snowball viburnum, 'Roseum,' is an old favorite with huge snowball shaped clusters of flowers. Unfortunately, this cultivar is also very attractive to aphids and they often cause the young tips to become distorted.

Sargent viburnum, also known as Sargent highbush viburnum, can become a large shrub, possibly 10 feet in height and spread. It has flat-topped clusters of white flowers in the spring with scarlet ⅜-inch fruits in the fall. The summer foliage color is light green, becoming a yellow or red in the fall. There is one commonly available cultivar called 'Onondaga' which becomes about half the mature size of the species. The foliage also has a maroon tinge. The flowers are similar to those of the species, but fruit production is sparse. It is more resistant to aphids than the European cranberrybush.

Viburnum lentago

American cranberrybush and its many cultivars are excellent plants for the landscape. The species may become 10 feet tall or more with an equal spread. The plant has clusters of flat-topped, white flowers. The fruit is about ⅓-inch in diameter, bright red, and remains through the winter. It is also edible and can be used to make jams and jellies. The leaves are green during the summer and turn a deep red in the fall. There are four popular cultivars commonly available. 'Alfredo' is a compact form, only reaching a mature height and spread of 5 or 6 feet. It also has an excellent red fall color.

Viburnum opulus 'nanum'

'Bailey Compact' is similar to Alfredo but has a deeper red fall color and glossy red fruit. It also tends to be slightly taller than broad and does not produce dependable flowers and fruit until the plant reaches maturity. The cultivar 'Hahs' is a slightly larger plant with a mature height and spread of 8 feet. It has large red fruit and a deep red fall color. 'Wentworth' is a heavy fruiting cultivar of American cranberrybush. It may become the same size as the species. American cranberrybush is native to South Dakota, being found in the northeast part of the state as well as the Black Hills.

Viburnums grow best in full-sun to part-sun locations. The ideal soil is slightly moist, well-drained, and slightly acidic. Viburnums will also tolerate an alkaline soil but not a wet or dry one.

Viburnums have few pest problems, but some, particularly the European cranberrybush and its cultivars, are susceptible to aphids and a foliage disease called anthracnose. Mildew may also occur in shaded locations.

Viburnum trilobum

Weigela

Old fashioned weigela   *Weigela florida*   Region 1,2,3,5

The weigela is probably best known as a flowering shrub, though several of the cultivars also have interesting foliage color. The pink to fuchsia flowers occur singly or in small clusters in the spring, but weigela also blooms sporadically throughout the summer and fall. The fruit is insignificant. The species has green foliage in the summer with no true fall color.

Weigela can become a medium-sized shrub with a mature height and spread of 5 to 6 feet. Many different cultivars of weigela are available. 'Variegated' has green leaves that are edged in pale yellow to creamy white. 'Java Red' has deep green leaves with a tinge of red. The flowers are a dark pink. It also is one of the smallest weigelas, reaching a mature height and spread of only 4 feet. 'Minuet' is even smaller, only becoming 2 or 3 feet tall. 'Pink Princess' is one of the showiest and has bright pink flowers and a long bloom period. It and 'Red Prince' are among the hardiest and rarely suffer serious tip dieback during our winters.

Weigela florida

Weigela florida

Weigela florida 'White Knight'

Weigelas are very adaptable but do best in a well-drained soil in a sunny location. They will tolerate alkaline soils. Weigelas may suffer some tip dieback during severe winters. They do require annual renewal pruning to look their best.

Vines for South Dakota

Vines are often an overlooked possibility in the residential landscape. They can be made to grow on a trellis or on the side of a wall or even a tree, as it is possible to find vines that will not damage walls or injure trees. Vines can have attractive flowers, interesting fruit, or even brilliant fall color.

Vines attach to supports in various ways, either twining or clinging to the support. Twining plants twine in different directions. If you are going to train a twining vine, start it from the correct direction. Bittersweet twines from left to right, while vining honeysuckle twines from right to left.

Twining plants are easy to remove from the support. Their one main difficulty is that they can strangle shrubs and small trees.

Clinging vines hold by tendrils that grip a support. Tendrils have disk-like hold-fasts or aerial rootlets. These grip tightly, so removal is difficult.

Hummingbird vine, Trumpetcreeper, Trumpet vine

Trumpetcreeper   *Campsis radicans*   Region 1,2,3,4,5

Campsis radicans

This is one of the toughest vines for our region. It has been said if you cannot grow this vine, you probably cannot grow anything on the site!

The common names trumpetcreeper and hummingbird vine refer to the best ornamental feature of the vine: the clusters of bright orange-scarlet, trumpet-shaped (2 to 3 inches long) flowers that occur from July to early September and are attractive to hummingbirds. Unfortunately, while the plant is hardy to our state, the flower buds can be killed by exposure to temperatures below -10 to -20 F. The flowers, if they occur, are followed by a 3-inch woody capsule that is neither showy nor objectionable. The foliage is green, turning to a yellow-green in the fall.

Trumpetcreeper can climb 30 feet up almost any object, be it a tree or brick wall. It clings to its support with aerial rootlets which attach very tightly. Because of this, it should not be planted against wooden walls. The best support is a trellis. However, due to the weight of the vine, the trellis must be sturdy.

Trumpetcreeper will grow in almost any soil from wet to dry and on soils with a wide range of pH. It performs best in full sun. While it is most hardy in the eastern portion of our state, it can be seen climbing chimneys in West River towns such as Murdo. In western locations it may die back if planted in the open. It is best planted along south-facing walls.

There are several cultivars of trumpetcreeper. 'Fava' is yellow to orange-yellow flowered, and 'Praecox' is red to orange-red flowered. There are also other species of trumpetcreeper, the Chinese (*C. grandifolia*) and a hybrid, *C. x tagliabuana*. However, neither is reliably hardy in South Dakota.

Bittersweet

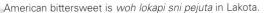

Chinese bittersweet	*Celastrus orbiculatus*	Region 1,2
American bittersweet	*Celastrus scandens*	Region 1-6

American bittersweet is *woh lokapi sni pejuta* in Lakota.

The unmistakable fruit is the primary ornamental value of the bittersweet vines. The fruit is a three-lobed capsule that has a yellow-orange shell surrounding a crimson red seed. It is frequently used in dried arrangements.

The flowers are not very showy. The leaves are a glossy green with a change to a yellow-green in the fall.

Bittersweets do not cling to structures for support but twine around objects. They are fast-growing vines and can girdle small trees and shrubs. Bittersweets can grow 20 feet or more if they have strong enough supports. They grow best in full sun but otherwise are tolerant of a wide range of soil conditions. Bittersweets are dioecious, which means that there are male and female plants. At least one male must be planted for every six females for good fruit set.

The better of the two to plant in South Dakota is our native American bittersweet. It is not as fast growing as the Chinese and is much hardier.

Celastrus scandens

Trumpet or Vining honeysuckle

Trumpet honeysuckle   *Lonicera sempervirens*   Region 1,2,3,5

Trumpet honeysuckle is an attractive vine with bluish-green leaves that have a purplish tinge when they first open. The 2-inch long flowers are tubular and scarlet with yellow-orange throats. They usually occur in clusters, bloom throughout the summer, and are very attractive to hummingbirds. The fruit is a small, ¼-inch, bright red berry.

Trumpet honeysuckle does not cling to a structure for support but instead twines around rails or laths. It can reach a height of 15 feet or more. It grows best in a full-sun location in a well-drained, neutral pH soil.

A closely related plant, the 'Dropmore Scarlet' honeysuckle, is hardier and also has outstanding orange-scarlet flowers.

Lonicera sempervirens

Shrubs for South Dakota

Virginia creeper, Woodbine

Parthenocissus quinquefolia

Parthenocissus tricuspidata

Virginia creeper	*Parthenocissus quinquefolia*	Region 1-6
Boston ivy	*Parthenocissus tricuspidata*	Region 1-6

The plant is *caniyuwi iyececa* in Lakota.

Virginia creeper is a vine with outstanding fall color. The leaflets can become a brilliant scarlet and crimson. The flowers are insignificant but the ¼-inch black berries are showy once the leaves fall.

This is a clinging vine that holds to its support with tendrils. It is the "ivy'" that graces many ivy league schools. Virginia creeper can grow to heights of 30 feet or more. It is an extremely tough plant, performing well in full sun to full shade and in all kinds of soil. The vine is susceptible to several scales and leafhoppers.

There are two varieties available. The Engelmann ivy (*P. quinquefolia* var. *engelmannii*) has smaller leaves than the species and a brighter fall color. It clings better to struc-

Parthenocissus quinquefolia

tures. The other variety, Saint-Paulii (*P. quinquefolia* var. *saint-paulii*), also has smaller leaves than the species and is more densely branched. It also has hold-fasts, so it is more tightly attached to any support.

The common name woodbine is more often applied to *P. inserta*, also known as thicket creeper. This is similar to the Virginia creeper but it does not have the hold-fasts. However, it does have tendrils.

Another related vine is the Boston ivy, *P. tricuspidata*. This vine has a three-lobed leaf rather than a palmately compound leaf. It has fall color and growth characteristics similar to the Virginia creeper. It also uses hold-fasts for support. Boston ivy is not as hardy, however, and may experience dieback if planted outside of Regions 1, 2, and the southern half of 5.

Parthenocissus tricuspidata

Conifer Evergreen Shrubs for South Dakota

Evergreens are an important feature in the South Dakota residential landscape. They provide a contrast to the deciduous foliage of other shrubs and give winter interest in an otherwise bare landscape. Unfortunately, they are often overused and are sometimes the only shrubs used.

A good rule-of-thumb is that evergreen shrubs, excluding evergreen groundcovers and herbaceous plants, should make up only about one third of the foundation landscape. This is usually enough greenery to provide winter interest, yet still allow adequate space for deciduous shrubs and herbaceous plants to give that much needed spring, summer, and fall color.

JUNIPER

Chinese juniper	*Juniperus chinensis*	Region 1-7
Common juniper	*Juniperus communis*	Region 1-7
Creeping juniper	*Juniperus horizontalis*	Region 1-7
Japgarden juniper	*Juniperus procumbens*	Region 1,2,3,5
Savin juniper	*Juniperus sabina*	Region 1-7
Rocky Mountain juniper	*Juniperus scopulorum*	Region 1-7
Eastern redcedar	*Juniperus virginiana*	Region 1-7

Junipers are our most common evergreen foundation plants. They are a very versatile group with a wide variety of shapes, colors, and sizes. Unfortunately, this same versatility means that the plants are frequently overused. It is not hard to find house foundation landscapes that are composed entirely of junipers.

Junipers are best planted in a full-sun location, but part sun is usually acceptable. If planted in an overly shaded location, they can become very open. The ideal soil is moist and well-drained, but junipers will grow in almost any soil except one that is wet. They are very pH adaptable. Junipers do have a number of serious pest problems, including twig blight and cedar-apple rust. They can be sheared anytime from March to July.

Chinese junipers range in habit from groundcovers to small trees. They have both scalelike and needlelike foliage that hold their color into the winter. The blue berry-like, fleshy cones are about ⅓-inch in diameter. Chinese junipers are moderately susceptible to twig blight but are rarely infected with cedar-apple rust. Some cultivars will suffer winter-burn.

Juniperus chinensis 'Mint Julep'

Cultivar	Foliage color	Shape	Height, Spread
Chinese juniper			
'Bakaurea'[1]	golden tipped	medium spreader	4 feet, 6 feet
'Maneyi'	bluish-green	medium spreader	4 feet, 5 feet
'Old Gold'	bronze-gold	low spreader	3 feet, 4 feet
'Mint Julep'	mint green	medium spreader	3 feet, 4 feet
'Ramlosa'	dark green	medium spreader	4 feet, 6 feet
var. sargentii[2]	blue green	groundcover	1-2 feet, 5 feet

[1] sold as Gold Star juniper®
[2] sold as Sargent juniper

Common junipers also have many different habits. The foliage is only needlelike and usually develops a yellow or brown cast during the winter. The berry-like cone is approximately ¼-inch in diameter. Common junipers are usually not infected with juniper twig blight, nor do they serve as alternate hosts of cedar-apple rust.

Juniperus communis var. depressa 'Vase'

Cultivar	Foliage color	Shape	Height, Spread
Common juniper			
'AmiDak'[1]	bright green	low spreader	2 feet, 4 feet
'Repanda'	silvery-green	low spreader	2 feet, 6 feet

[1] sold as Blueberry Delight juniper.® (The name is due to its heavy production of berry-like cones.)

Creeping juniper is always low-growing. The foliage may be either scalelike or needlelike. The summer color is bright green to bluish-green which may turn a purple or brown during the winter. The berry-like cones are ¼-inch in diameter. It is moderately susceptible to twig blight, but rarely serves as an alternate host to cedar-apple rust.

Juniperus horizontalis 'Blue Chip'

Cultivar	Foliage color	Shape	Height, Spread
Creeping juniper			
'BelDak'[1]	silvery-green	groundcover	1 foot, 4 feet
'BowDak'[2]	bright green	groundcover	1 foot, 4 feet
'Blue Chip'	blue	groundcover	1 foot, 6 feet
'Hughes'	silvery-blue	groundcover	1 foot, 8 feet
'Prince of Wales'	bright green	groundcover	½ foot, 4 feet
'Webberi'	bluish-green	groundcover	½ foot, 4 feet
'Wiltoni'	blue	groundcover	½ foot, 4 feet

[1] sold as Prairie Mist®
[2] sold as Prairie Elegance®

Shrubs for South Dakota

Japgarden juniper is usually low-growing. The foliage may be either scalelike or needle-like. Summer color is a light bluish-green. The foliage tips turn a light bronzy-pink in the winter. The plant is resistant to twig blight and cedar-apple rust.

Cultivar	Foliage color	Shape	Height, Spread
Japgarden juniper			
'Nana'[1]	bluish-green	groundcover	½ foot, 4 feet

[1] sold as Dwarf Japgarden juniper

Juniperus procumbens

Juniperus sabina 'Broadmoor'

Savin junipers are primarily shrubs. The foliage may be either scalelike or needlelike and usually has a pungent odor when crushed. The berry-like cones are violet and about ¼-inch in diameter. The species is very resistant to twig blight and rarely serves as a host to cedar-apple rust.

Cultivar	Foliage color	Shape	Height, Spread
Savin juniper			
'Arcadia'	green	groundcover	1-2 feet, 4 feet
'Broadmoor'	grayish-green	low mounding	3 feet, 6 feet
'Buffalo'	bright green	groundcover	1 foot, 5 feet
'Monna'[1]	light green	groundcover	1 foot, 5 feet
'Monard'[2]	grayish-green	low mounding	2 feet, 5 feet
'Pepin'	blue-green	low spreader	3 feet, 4 feet

[1] sold as Calgary Carpet, Mini-Arcade, or Mini-Arcadia
[2] sold as Moor-Dense

Rocky Mountain juniper generally is a tree, but there are a few shrub types. The plant has scalelike foliage that is usually green to light blue. The color often fades slightly in the winter, but Rocky Mountain junipers usually maintain better winter color than other junipers. The blue berry-like cones are about ¼-inch in diameter. Rocky Mountain junipers are very susceptible to twig blight and cedar-apple rust.

Cultivar	Foliage color	Shape	Height, Spread
Rocky Mountain juniper			
'Medora'	blue-green	columnar	10 feet, 6 feet
'Sutherland'	silvery-green	pyramidal	15 feet, 10 feet
'Table Top'	silvery-blue	medium spreader	4 feet, 5 feet
'Welchi'	bluish-green	columnar	8 feet, 4 feet

Eastern redcedar is also usually a tree, but there are a few shrub types. The plant may have scalelike or needlelike foliage. The summer color is green but may turn purple to brown during the winter. The blue, berry-like cones are about ¼-inch in diameter. Eastern redcedar is very susceptible to juniper twig blight and cedar-apple rust.

Cultivar	Foliage color	Shape	Height, Spread
Eastern redcedar			
'Canaertii'	dark rich green	pyramidal	15 feet, 10 feet
'Gray Owl'	silvery-gray	low spreader	2 feet, 4 feet
'Taylor'	medium green	columnar	10 feet, 4 feet

Juniperus scopulorum 'Medora'

Juniperus virginiana 'Gray Owl'

Shrubs for South Dakota

Russian-cypress

Russian-cypress   *Microbiota decussata*   Region 1-6

Russian-cypress is a relatively new introduction from eastern Siberia. The scalelike foliage resembles arborvitae, but the growth habit is similar to a groundcover juniper. The foliage is a bright green in the summer but develops a brown cast during the winter. The plant is about 1 foot tall with a spread of 4 feet. It will tolerate more shade than a juniper, otherwise its growing requirements are similar. It is very hardy in South Dakota. There is one cultivar available called 'Northern Pride.' Its winter color is more bronze than brown, otherwise it is similar to the species.

Microbiota decussata

Yew

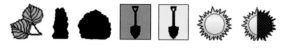

Japanese yew   *Taxus cuspidata*   Region 1,2,5
Anglojap yew   *Taxus* x *media*   Region 1,2,5

Taxus x media

Yews are considered to be the finest of all the evergreen foundation plants. They have soft, rich, dark green foliage that responds well to shearing. Yews also have a dense growth habit. They can be sheared anytime from March to July.

The fleshy seed covering is berrylike, about ¼-inch in diameter and bright red. Yews have separate sexes so the seed is only found on female plants and many cultivars are only males. The seeds are highly poisonous to humans and animals.

Taxus cuspidata

Japanese yew is not commonly seen in South Dakota landscapes as it is not reliably hardy. There is one cultivar, 'Capitata,' that can be found in some areas of the state that have a milder climate. It is usually sold as an upright or pyramidal yew and can reach a height of 10 to 12 feet with a spread of 6 feet at the base.

Several Anglojap yew cultivars are planted in South Dakota. The most common is the 'Tauntonii' or Taunton spreading yew. This is a very hardy yew that has a compact spreading habit. It can reach a height of 3 or 4 feet with a spread of 4 or 5 feet. The 'Dark Green' yew may become a little larger than the Taunton yew and is not quite as hardy.

Yews should be planted on a north or east exposure in South Dakota to protect them from the winter sun. If possible, they should also receive some protection from the winter winds to reduce the chance of winter-burn. While yews will tolerate slightly alkaline soils, they will not tolerate poorly drained soils. Yews require soils that are well drained.

Arborvitae, White cedar

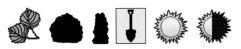

American arborvitae   *Thuja occidentalis*   Region 1,2,3,5,6

Arborvitaes are excellent evergreen foundation plants. The soft, fanlike foliage can be very attractive. Unfortunately, arborvitae foliage often develops a brown cast during the winter and winter-burn is a possibility on windy or exposed sites. Many cultivars are available with a wide variety of mature sizes and shapes. The following are some of the possibilities for the residential landscape.

Cultivar	Foliage color	Shape	Height
'Brandon'	soft green	compact pyramidal	12 feet
'Hetz Midget'	rich green	compact globe	2 feet
'Holmstrup'	bright green	compact pyramidal	4 feet
'Little Gem'	dark green	informal mound	3 feet
'Little Giant'	bright green	dense globe	5 feet
'Rushmore'	dark green	narrow upright	15 feet
'Sherwood Moss'	soft green	broad globe	4 feet
'Techny'	very dark green	pyramidal	12 feet
'Woodwardii'[1]	dark green	globe	5 feet

[1] Sold as Woodward

The 'Techny' arborvitae is also available in a globe form sold as the 'Techny Globe' arborvitae. However, unless the plant continues to be sheared into a globe shape, it will revert to its more pyramidal form. 'Rushmore' is a South Dakota State University introduction.

Arborvitaes do best in a full-sun to part-sun location. Most need protection from the winter sun, so east exposures are probably the best site for South Dakota landscapes. They should be planted on moist, well-drained soils but are tolerant of alka-line conditions. The primary prob-lem associated with growing arborvi-taes in South Dakota is winter. Winter sun and harsh wind may result in winter burn or dieback. Heavy snow or ice loads may cause the plant to split. Arborvitaes can be sheared from March to July.

Thuja occidentalis

Other Dwarf Conifers

*While junipers, yews, and arborvitaes are our most common evergreen shrubs,
there are numerous dwarf forms of pine and spruce available for the residential
landscape. The following is a a sample of varieties that can be planted.*

Spruce

Spruce produces single, 4-sided needles. They generally do best in full-sun
locations and on well-drained soil. Tree forms of spruce are covered in
Extension Circular 903, *Trees for South Dakota.* The following are some of
the more common dwarf spruce available at garden centers. These plants
should receive protection from the winter sun and wind to avoid winter-burn. They also frequently have problems with spider mites. Spruce should be sheared in late summer to fall.

Birdnest spruce   *Picea abies* 'Nidiformis'   Region 1,2,5

This is a flat-topped spreading conifer with a mature height of 2 or 3 feet and a spread of 3
to 5 feet.

Dwarf Alberta spruce   *Picea glauca* 'Conica'   Region 1,2,5

This is a very slow growing, compact, pyramidal evergreen. The mature size is about 5 feet
with a base of 3 feet, but plants rarely achieve this size in South Dakota.

Shrubs for South Dakota

Dwarf Norway spruce   *Picea abies* 'Pumila'   Region 1,2,5

This is similar to the Birdnest spruce, except the foliage is more light to reddish-brown. The mature size is a height of about 2 feet and a spread of 3 feet.

Dwarf Serbian spruce   *Picea omorika* 'Nana'   Region 1,2,5

This is a slow-growing conifer with a mature height of 6 feet. The form is conical to globose and the foliage is a bright green.

Montgomery blue spruce   *Picea pungens* 'Montgomery'   Region 1,2,3,5,6

Montgomery is a slow-growing, broadly pyramidal form of blue spruce. The mature height and spread are about 5 feet. The needle color is a bright blue.

Picea abies 'Pumila'

Picea omorika 'Nana'

Picea pungens 'Montgomery'

Pine

Mugo pine   *Pinus mugo*   Region 1-7

Pines produce needles in clusters of 2, 3, or 5 depending upon the species. They are best planted in a full-sun location and on well-drained soils. For more information on pine identification or culture see Extension Circular 903, Trees for South Dakota.

Mugo pine can be a low-growing shrub to a medium-sized tree depending upon the variety or cultivar selected. It is important to pick a cultivar that achieves the size appropriate for its use in the landscape. 'Big Tuna' is a broad, upright mugo pine with a mature height of 6 feet. 'Slowmound' becomes a dense mound about 3 feet tall at maturity. However, there is still a great variation in mature height and spread, and this plant should be used with caution in small, confining spaces. Mugo pine, as with all pine, should only be sheared when candling, when the new shrubs are expanding.

Pinus mugo

Selected Lists of Plants With Various Adaptive or Ornamental Characteristics

The hardiest shrubs

These are most tolerant of harsh, windy winter conditions.

Buffaloberry	Clove currant	Common lilac
Coralberry	Creeping juniper	Late lilac
Potentilla	Siberian peashrub	Snowberry
Tamarix	Tatarian dogwood	

Shrubs that best tolerate shady locations

Almost all shrubs perform best in full sun. Planting in shady locations, those receiving less than 6 hours of direct sun, will generally result in a shrub that produces fewer flowers and poorer fall color in comparison to the same plant growing in a sunny location. The following shrubs are least affected by shade.

Chokeberries	Dwarf Korean boxwood	Elderberries
Fiveleaf aralia	Snowberries	Viburnums
Yews		

Shrubs that best tolerate very alkaline soils

Almost every shrub does best in a soil that is slightly acid. These shrubs are most tolerant of highly alkaline soils. Some chlorosis (yellowing leaves) may still occur, particularly if the soils are above a pH of 8.0 or are poorly drained.

Bristly locust	Buffaloberry	Fiveleaf aralia
Honeysuckle	Siberian peashrub	

Shrubs that best tolerate poorly-drained soils

Shrubs do best on a well-drained soil. These can best tolerate poorly drained, clay soils. However, in such soils flowering may be reduced and the plants may have more winter injury.

American cranberrybush	Arrowwood viburnum	Elderberries
Red chokeberry	Redosier dogwood	Tatarian dogwood

Shrubs for formal hedges

While almost any shrub can be used as a screen or hedge, these shrubs respond best to shearing and best maintain a formal appearance.

Alpine currant	Dwarf Arctic blue willow	Dwarf Korean boxwood
Dwarf ninebark	European fly honeysuckle	Hedge cotoneaster
Japanese barberry	Yews	

Shrubs and vines with the best fall color

Fall color can be an important feature in the South Dakota landscape. These shrubs that have most brilliant fall color. Coloration is generally best if the shrub is growing in a well-drained soil in a sunny location.

American cranberrybush (red)
Chokeberries (red)
Serviceberries (red and yellow)
Staghorn sumac (red and yellow)

Bittersweet (yellow)
Fragrant sumac (red)
Smooth sumac (red)

Burning bush (red)
Korean barberry (red)
Woodbine (red)

Shrubs with fragrant flowers

While many shrubs have a slight fragrance, these are the best.

Butterfly bush
Daphne
Tatarian honeysuckle

Clove currant
Koreanspice viburnum

Common lilac
Mockorange

Native shrubs

The following is a list of plants native to South Dakota. However, our state is one of extremes. Shrubs native to the upper elevations of the Black Hills, while native to our state, are not necessarily better adapted to Britton, for example, than any other plant. Because of the difference in growing conditions between mountains and prairies, we have formulated two lists.

Black Hills region

American cranberrybush
Creeping mahonia
Redosier dogwood
Smooth sumac

Common juniper
Fragrant sumac
Rocky Mountain juniper

Creeping juniper
Mountain ninebark
Saskatoon serviceberry

Prairies

American bittersweet
Buffalo currant
Gray dogwood
Nannyberry viburnum
Silver buffaloberry

American cranberrybush
Eastern redcedar
Hairy honeysuckle
Potentilla
Virginia creeper

American elderberry
Eastern wahoo
Juneberry
Redosier dogwood
Wolfberry

Summer Keys of Common South Dakota Shrubs

These keys are designed to allow you to systematically identify a shrub by observing various plant parts. It is best to use a key where the shrub is growing, for then, all the characteristics of the shrub are handy for checking against the key. If this is not possible, a good branch sample with leaves attached is necessary. Having samples of the flowers or fruit is also very helpful.

A key can be compared to a road sign where a choice of two directions must be made at an intersection. In this key, two alternatives are given for each number. Which of the two to select depends on how well the descriptions fit the characteristics of the shrub in question. Only one o the two choices will normally fit. Always start with the number one choice and proceed down the key until the shrub is named. If you find that neither choice makes sense, a wrong choice was made in an earlier step. Backtrack to see where an incorrect choice was made.

Suppose you are examining a shrub that has broad, thin leaves and is deciduous. The leaves are simple and opposite and not lobed. The leaves are also entire and silver scales cover them. The branches have 1- to 2-inch spines. The first step is to decide which of the five keys to use. Starting with #1 immediately below, decide which choice matches the features of the shrub in question. 1b fits since the leaves are broad and thin and deciduous. Now go to #2 (as indicated at the end of the line). Choice 2a fits because the leaves are opposite; go to #3. At 3, choice 3a is the one you want since the leaves are simple; so now you know Key 2 is where you go next.

At Key 2 go to #1 and compare the choices offered. Choice 1b is correct because the leaves are not lobed; that choice directs you to #4 in Key 2. At 4 the correct choice is 4a because the leaves are entire; go to #5. At #5 the correct choice is 5a because the leaves are covered with silvery scales and branches are spiny, 1-2 inches long. At the end of the line the plant identified is silver buffaloberry. Turn to page 51 for pictures and more information about this plant. If you need help understanding some of the terminology, consult the glossary on p. 101.

1a. Leaves needle-, awl- or scale-like .... **Key**
 b. Leaves broad and thin, deciduous ....

2a. Leaves opposite ....
 b. Leaves alternate ....

3a. Leaves simple .... **Key**
 b. Leaves compound .... **Key**

4a. Leaves simple .... **Key**
 b. Leaves compound .... **Key**

Key 1. Shrubs with needlelike, awl-like or scale-like leaves

1a. Leaves needlelike ....
 b. Leaves awl-like or scale-like...

2a. Needles are flat..
 b. Needles are not flat ....

3a. Needles have two yellowish or grayish green bands beneath,
   conspicuous midrib, leathery .... **Yew** (p. 82)
b. Needles have two pale bluish or whitish
   bands beneath, not leathery .... **Serbian spruce** (p. 85)

4a. Needles attached to the twig in fascicles of 2 or more .... **Pine** (p. 86)
b. Needles attached singly to twig, 4-sided .... **Spruce** (p. 84)

5a. Leaves deciduous, alternate .... **Tamarisk** (p. 62)
b. Leaves evergreen, opposite 6

6a. Leaves awl-like or scale-like and not overlapping,
   cones berry-like.. **Juniper** (p. 76)
b. Leaves scale-like and overlapping, cones dry at maturity 7

7a. Branchlets soft, fan-like in one plane; leaves overlapping
   in 4 rows .... **Arborvitae** (p. 83)
b. Branchlets more or less flattened, 4-sided; leaves
   very small, triangular.. **Russian-cypress** (p. 81)

Key 2. Shrubs with opposite, simple leaves

1a. Leaves are lobed.. 2
b. Leaves are not lobed 4

2a. Petiole with a very deep groove, with large
   disk-like glands pink-reddish in color .... **Sargent viburnum** (p. 63)
b. Petiole with a shallow groove 3

3a. Leaves hairy beneath; petiole with a few large
   disk-like, conclave glands................................. **European cranberrybush** (p. 63)
b. Leaves without hairs; petiole with small
   dome-shaped stalked glands .... **American cranberrybush** (p. 63)

4a. Leaves entire 5
b. Leaves serrate... 23

5a. Leaves covered with silvery scales; branches
   spiny, 1-2 inches long... **Silver buffaloberry** (p. 51)
b. Leaves not covered with silvery scales, branches not spiny................................. 6

6a. Leaves leathery and evergreen .... **Korean boxwood** (p. 17)
b. Leaves not leathery and deciduous 7

7a. Leaves with lateral veins parallel to the margin 8
b. Leaves without lateral veins parallel to the margin 10

8a. Leaves wedge-shaped at base; stem tan to
reddish brown.. **Gray dogwood** (p. 19)
b. Leaves rounded at base; stem other than above.. 9

9a. Leaf ending in a slender tip; young stem
becoming dark blood red... **Redosier dogwood** (p. 19)
b. Leaf ending in an acute tip, bullate above; young stem
becoming deep red .... **Tatarian dogwood** (p. 19)

10a. Leaves obovate-lanceolate, less than ⅜ inch wide; twigs
with minute hairs.. **Common privet** (p. 31)
b. Leaves not lanceolate, more than ⅜ inch wide; twigs not as above..................... 11

11a. Leaf base cordate, subcordate, or cuneate 12
b. Leaf base not cordate, subcordate, or cuneate 16

12a. Leaves pubescent on at least midrib 13
b. Leaves not pubescent 14

13a. Leaf tip acuminate, cuneate.. **Manchurian lilac** (p. 59)
b. Leaf tip obtuse or abruptly acuminate 14

14a. Leaves medium green above and gray-green
below, cuneate .... **Littleleaf lilac** (p. 59)
b. Leaves dark green above and pale below 15

15a. Leaves 2-6 inches long, acute at ends; veins impressed.............. **Late lilac** (p. 59)
b. Leaves 1-2 inches long, acute base; reddish-purple margin
around young leaves .... **Meyer lilac** (p. 59)

16a. Leaves broad-ovate or ovate.. 17
b. Leaves oblong to oblong-lanceolate 18

17a. Leaves broad-ovate, turning reddish-purple in the fall .... **Hyacinth lilac** (p. 59)
b. Leaves ovate, subcordate, dark to bluish green .... **Common lilac** (p. 59)

18a. Leaves green above and gray-green beneath .... **Preston lilac** (p. 59)
b. Leaves dark green, cuneate .... **Chinese lilac** (p. 59)

19a. Single bundle scar... 20
b. Three bundle scars 21

20a. Leaves oval to elliptic-oblong, often sinuately lobed;
pith excavated .... **White snowberry** (p. 57)
b. Leaves elliptic to ovate; pith continuous .... **Coralberry** (p. 57)

21a. Stem a vine; uppermost pair of leaves on stem
      usually envelop stem.. **Vining honeysuckle** (p. 72)
   b. Stem not a vine 22

22a. Leaves dark green above, bluish green below;
      stem green turning to brown.................................. **Tatarian honeysuckle** (p. 32)
   b. Leaves dark grayish green; stem hairy, gray .... **European fly honeysuckle** (p. 32)

23a. Terminal bud a modified spine; twigs appearing
      subopposite.. **Common buckthorn** (p. 41)
   b. Terminal bud not a modified spine; twigs opposite............................. 24

24a. Twig pith chambered, though may be solid at nodes.................. **Forsythia** (p. 27)
   b. Twig pith solid 25

25a. Twigs with rows of hairs... 26
   b. Twigs with either hairs, though not in rows, or smooth 27

26a. Twigs with two rows of hairs running either side; petiole hairy;
      leaf margins not hairy... **Weigela** (p. 67)
   b. Twigs with 4 rows of hairs on a ridge joining
      the petiole base; petiole not hairy; leaf
      margins fringed with tiny hairs.......................... **Dwarf bush-honeysuckle** (p. 24)

27a. Petioles very short or nearly lacking 28
   b. Petiole about ⅛ inch or longer.. 29

28a. Twigs with 4 conspicuous wings; leaves obovate,
      1-3 inches, green beneath .... **Burning bush** (p. 25)
   b. Twigs without wings, but 4-angled and downy; leaves
      lanceolate, 4-10 inches long, white-tomentose beneath....... **Butterfly bush** (p. 16)

29a. Leaves ovate to elliptic-ovate or oblong-ovate, cuneate base............................. 30
   b. Leaves not as above, cordate base 33

30a. Petiole usually winged with a wavy margin;
      leaves lustrous dark green; buds long and curved.................. **Nannyberry** (p. 63)
   b. Petiole not winged; leaves and buds not as above................................... 31

31a. Leaves with stiff hairs beneath; stem reddish-brown
      with gray vertical streaks............................... **Panicle hydrangea** (p. 29)
   b. Leaves nearly hairless above, downy beneath especially
      along veins; stems not streaked.. 32

32a. Teeth on leaves remote, perhaps only 7 to a side;
      older stems with shredding bark .... **Sweet mockorange** (p. 35)
  b. Teeth on leaves very fine; stems 4-angled with
      corky lines .... **Eastern wahoo** (p. 25)

33a. Leaves have clusters of down above and more
      dense below, wrinkled above .... **Wayfaring tree** (p. 63)
  b. Leaves with minute hairs beneath,
      not wrinkled .... **Hills-of-snow hydrangea** (p. 29)

Key 3. Shrubs with opposite, pinnately compound leaves

1a. Stem a climbing vine with aerial rootlets,
     9-11 leaflets .... **Trumpetcreeper** (p. 70)
  b. Stem not a climbing vine, fewer leaflets ....

2a. Twig pith usually white, usually 7 leaflets .... **American elderberry** (p. 50)
  b. Twig pith usually brown, usually 5-7 leaflets .... **European red elder** (p. 50)

Key 4. Shrubs with alternate, simple leaves

1a. Leaves lobed ....
  b. Leaves not lobed ....

2a. Stem a climbing vine .... **Boston ivy** (p. 74)
  b. Stem not a climbing vine ....

3a. Bark near base of stems separating into thin layers ....
  b. Bark near base of stem not separating into thin layers ....

4a. Lobes are deeply cut, 3-lobed,
     leaves ¾-1½ inches long .... **Mountain ninebark** (p. 37)
  b. Lobes not deeply cut, usually 5-lobed,
     leaves 1-3 inches long ....**Common ninebark** (p. 37)

5a. Twig is slender and smooth, zig-zaggy ....
  b. Twig is coarser, sometimes having ridges running from leaf scar ....

6a. Leaves roundish, usually 3-lobed .... **Threelobe spirea** (p. 53)
  b. Leaves somewhat obovate, may be 3-5 lobed .... **Vanhoutee spirea** (p. 53)

7a. Middle lobe sides are convex, 3-5 lobed; stems
    gray-brown with short soft hairs .... **Clove currant** (p. 47)
  b. Middle lobe sides not convex, lobes 3, rarely 5;
    stems light brown with conspicuous ridges........................ **Alpine currant** (p. 47)

8a. Leaf margin entire 9
  b. Leaf margin serrate 17

9a. Leaves more or less leathery and persistent 10
  b. Leaves not leathery 11

10a. Leaves ½-1 inch long, oblanceolate, lustrous dark
     green above, glaucous beneath.................................... **Burkwood daphne** (p. 23)
   b. Leaves 1-3 inches long, oblong, dark green in
     summer becoming purplish in fall........................... **P.J.M. rhododendron** (p. 44)

11a. Stems with spines, angled between nodes.. 12
   b. Stems without spines, not angled between nodes.............................. 13

12a. Inner bark yellow; leaves bright green above .... **Japanese barberry** (p. 14)
   b. Inner bark not yellow; leaves silvery-scaly........................ **Sea buckthorn** (p. 28)

13a. Leaf veins parallel to the margin 14
   b. Leaf veins not parallel to the margin 15

14a. Leaves pale or whitish and hairy beneath,
     elliptic ovate, 2-5 inches long, 5-6 pairs of veins,
     petiole 1-2 inches long.. **Pagoda dogwood** (p. 19)
   b. Leaves light green and hairless or somewhat
     hairy on veins beneath, obovate, 1-3 inches long,
     8-9 pairs of veins, petiole ¼-½ inch long .... **Glossy buckthorn** (p. 41)

15a. Leaf petiole about half the blade length;
     stems purplish-brown with prominent
     lenticels; pith orange-brown .... **Smokebush** (p. 21)
   b. Leaf petiole less than half the blade length 16

16a. Leaves are hairy beneath, margins somewhat fringed
     with hairs; stems finely hairy .... **Azalea** (p. 43)
   b. Leaves have only sparse hairs beneath, no hairs on
     margins; stems hairy when young, peeling later.......... **Hedge cotoneaster** (p. 22)

17a. Stem with spines, flat with 1-5 lobes .... **Korean barberry** (p. 14)
   b. Stem without spines 18

18a. Stem a climbing vine .... **Bittersweet** (p. 71)
   b. Stem not a climbing vine 19

19a. Leaves reddish-purple; petiole with one or
     more glands at the upper end .... **Purpleleaf sand cherry** (p. 40)
  b. Leaves green-blue green; petiole without glands 20

20a. Leaves with blackish glands on midrib above 21
  b. Leaves without blackish glands 22

21a. Leaves with grayish wooly hairs beneath, margins set
     with black-tipped teeth; stem tomentose .... **Red chokeberry** (p. 12)
  b. Leaves smooth or nearly so beneath, margins
     without black-tipped teeth; stems without hairs .... **Black chokeberry** (p. 12)

22a. Leaf base broad, cordate or nearly so 23
  b. Leaf base acute or tapering 24

23a. Leaves with hairs, especially near cordate base .... **Apple serviceberry** (p. 10)
  b. Leaves without hairs, base subcordate .... **Allegeny serviceberry** (p. 10)

24a. Bud covered with a single scale; stems
     purplish turning to gray .... **Dwarf Arctic blue willow** (p. 49)
  b. Bud covered with several scales; stems not as above 25

25a. Leaves lanceolate or nearly so 26
  b. Leaves not lanceolate 27

26a. Leaves coarsely but singly serrated, dark green
     above, bluish green beneath .... **Japanese white spirea** (p. 53)
  b. Leaves finely and doubly serrated, purplish when
     young turning dark green .... **Bumalda spirea** (p. 53)

27a. Leaves oblong to oblanceolate 28
  b. Leaves not oblong or oblanceolate, but instead ovate, obovate, or elliptic 29

28a. Leaves hairy beneath, 1-3 inches long;
     petiole ⅛ inch long .... **Japanese spirea** (p. 53)
  b. Leaves not hairy beneath, 1-1½ inches long; no petiole .... **Garland spirea** (p. 53)

29a. Leaves elliptic, denticulate, dark green
     lustrous above, hairy beneath .... **Bridalwreath spirea** (pp. 53)
  b. Leaves ovate or orbicular 30

30a. Leaf tip crenate, obovate, dark blue-green .... **Nippon spirea** (p. 53)
  b. Leaf tip not crenate, other than above 31

31a. Leaves roundish, usually 3-lobed .... **Threelobe spirea** (p. 53)
  b. Leaves somewhat obovate, may be 3-5 lobed .... **Vanhoutte spirea** (p. 53)

Key 5. Shrubs with alternate, compound leaves

1a. Leaves palmately compound.. 2
  b. Leaves pinnately compound.. 3

2a. Stem a climbing vine with branched tendrils,
     5 stalked leaflets... **Virginia creeper** (p. 73)
  b. Stem not a vine .... **Fiveleaf aralia** (p. 9)

3a. Leaves leathery and evergreen, 3-7 leaflets .... **Creeping mahonia** (p. 34)
  b. Leaves not leathery and deciduous 4

4a. Leaflets usually 5 or fewer.. 5
  b. Leaflets usually 7 or more 6

5a. Leaflets usually 3, terminal leaflet twice as large
     as lateral.. **Fragrant sumac** (p. 45)
  b. Leaflets usually 5, leaflets more or less of uniform size............. **Potentilla** (p. 38)

6a. Leaflet margins entire 7
  b. Leaflet margins serrate... 8

7a. Leaves even-pinnate compound, 8-12 leaflets;
     stem with short soft hairs.............................. **Siberian peashrub** (p. 18)
  b. Leaves odd-pinnate compound, 7-13 leaflets; stems
     and petioles covered with stiff bristly hairs .... **Bristly locust** (p. 48)

8a. Stipules present; twigs fine; 13-23 leaflets;
     pith large, brown, continuous............................ **Ural falsespirea** (p. 52)
  b. Stipules absent; twigs stout... 9

9a. Branchlets hairy, leaf scars "c" shaped;
     13-27 leaflets .... **Staghorn sumac** (p. 45)
  b. Branchlets not hairy, somewhat 3-sided, leaf scar
     horse-shoe shaped; 11-31 leaflets .... **Smooth sumac** (p. 45)

Glossary

Alternate	describing leaves arranged with only a single leaf at each node.
Acuminate	the apex is gradually concave and tapers to a point.
Awl-like	tapered from the base to a slender and stiff point.
Blade	the flat, expanded portion of the leaf.
Bract	a modified, much-reduced leaf attached below a fruit or flower.
Bullate	the surface between the veins appears blistered.
Bundle scar	woody vascular area that connected the stem and leaf.
Capsule	a dry fruit that splits when ripe along two or more lines to release seeds.
Catkin	an unbranched, elongated main stem whose unisexual flowers have very short flower stalks.
Chlorotic	yellowish leaves; frequently the veins will be yellow and tissue between veins will be yellowish.
Compound leaf	a leaf with two or more completely separate blade segments (referred to as leaflets).
Cone	a seed-bearing structure with woody, overlapping scales. Male cones are produced, too, but aren't woody.
Crenate	rounded teeth on the margin.
Cultivar	a cultivated plant that is selected from a species, propagated for horticultural purposes, and which, when reproduced, maintains its distinguishing characteristic(s).
Cordate	heart shaped.
Corymb	an unbranched, elongated main stem whose flowers have stalks of unequal lengths, forming a flat-topped cluster of flowers.
Cuneate	wedge shaped. Attached at the narrow end.
Deciduous	trees that shed their leaves in the fall.
Dioecious	a plant that has only male or female flowers appearing on separate plants.
Divergent	spreading apart from a common base.
Double	a flower with more than twice the number of petals that normally occur.
Doubly pinnate	leaflets of a compound leaf are compound again.
Doubly serrate	the teeth on the leaf margin divided into finer teeth.
Drupe	a fleshy fruit with a pit or stone.

Eliptical	broad at the middle, narrow at each end.
Entire	a leaf margin with a smooth, rather than toothed, edge.
Even-pinnate	compound leaves that have two opposite leaflets at the tip.
Fascicle	a cluster or bundle of needles.
Gland	any small protuberance or knob-like structure.
Habit	the overall shape of the tree.
Hold-fasts	fine rootlike structures tht some vines use for attachment.
Honeydew	a sticky secretion from aphids, scale, or related insects, often turning black when infected by a fungus.
Lanceolate	much longer than wide. Broadest below the middle and tapering to an apex.
Leaf scar	scar left on the stem by a falling leaf.
Leaf scorch	the browning of the leaf margin. This may be due to environmental conditions such as droughts or bacteria.
Leaflet	a leaf-like structure which with other leaflets makes up a compound leaf. The lack of a bud at the base of the leaflets and the presence of a bud at the base of the compound leaf can be used to tell whether you are looking at a leaflet or a leaf.
Lenticel	a small corky area consisting of cells providing gas exchange. Found on young bark.
Lobe	a portion of a leaf blade defined by a relatively deep indentation in the blade.
Lustrous	a slight metallic gloss.
Midvein	the central or main vein of a leaf.
Native	a plant growing naturally in a particular area without the intervention of people.
Monoecious	a plant that has both male and female flowers on the same plant.
Node	the particular location on the stem that bears a leaf or leaves.
Oblong	longer than broad, margins nearly parallel.
Obovate	egg-shaped in outline, with the narrowest portion at the basal end.
Odd-pinnately compound	compound leaves that have a single leaflet at the tip.
Opposite	having two leaves at a single node, one on each side of the twig.
Oval	a somewhat flattened circle.
Ovate	egg-shaped in outline, with the broadest portion at the basal end.

Palmate	radiating from a common center somewhat like spokes on a wheel.
Palmately compound	a compound leaf where the leaflets have a single, common point of attachment.
Panicle	a branched main stem with side branches bearing loose clusters of flowers.
Persistent	remaining attached.
Petiole	the stalk of a leaf.
Petiolule	the stalk of a leaflet.
Pinnae	leaflets or rows of leaflets attached along the rachis of a pinnately compound leaf.
Pinnate	arranged like individual divisions of a feather.
Pinnately compound	a compound leaf having the leaflets attached along both sides of a common central stalk (the rachis).
Pith	the central part of a twig.
Pod	a dry fruit that splits open along one or two lines (sutures).
Pome	a fleshy fruit with a central core, e. g. an apple or pear.
Pubescent	covered with fine, soft hairs.
Raceme	an unbranched, elongated main stem whose flowers have stalks that are all about the same length.
Rachis	the central stalk of a compound leaf.
Rootstock	the portion of a grafted plant which makes up the root system.
Saline	with a high salt content.
Samara	a dry, one-seeded, winged fruit.
Scale	the spirally arranged, modified leaves of a cone or leaf bud.
Scalelike	small, flattened, often with a pointed tip.
Semi-double	a flower with more that normal number of petals but less than double the number.
Serrate	with saw-like teeth on the margin of the leaf.
Sessile	the leaf blade or leaflet lacking a stalk.
Simple	one continuous piece.
Sinus	the gap between two lobes.
Stipules	basal appendage of a petiole.
Subopposite	leaves closely paired, but not exactly opposite one another

Sucker	a shoot arising from the roots. Suckers from rootstocks do not exhibit the same ornamental characteristics (ie white flowers, red fruits etc.) as the cultivar.
Terminal	at the distal end; tip.
Thorn	a reduced, sharp-pointed branch.
Tomentosa	densely wooly; soft/matted hairs.
Unisexual	flowers that are either male or female.
Variety	a plant found in nature that differs from other members of the species in one or more characteristics and maintains these distinguishing characteristics when reproduced by seed.
Whorled	describing a group of three or more leaves that radiate out from the same node of a branch.
Winter injury	any plant injury that can be attributed to winter weather.

Flower types

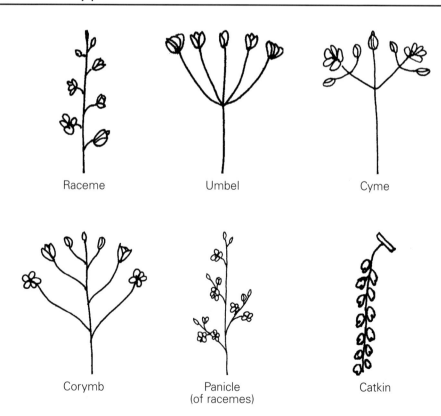

Raceme   Umbel   Cyme

Corymb   Panicle   Catkin
(of racemes)

Leaf shapes and margins

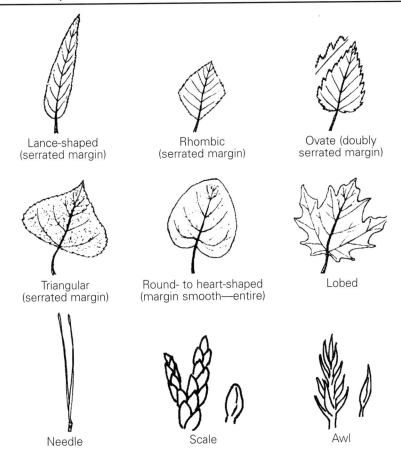

Lance-shaped
(serrated margin)

Rhombic
(serrated margin)

Ovate (doubly
serrated margin)

Triangular
(serrated margin)

Round- to heart-shaped
(margin smooth—entire)

Lobed

Needle

Scale

Awl

Leaf and bud arrangement

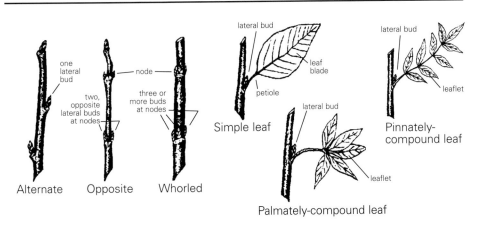

one
lateral
bud

node

two,
opposite
lateral buds
at nodes

three or
more buds
at nodes

Alternate

Opposite

Whorled

lateral bud

leaf
blade

petiole

Simple leaf

lateral bud

leaflet

Palmately-compound leaf

lateral bud

leaflet

Pinnately-
compound leaf

Leaf shapes and margins; leaf and bud arrangement

Common Name Index

Aralia 9
    Fiveleaf 9, 88, 99
Arborvitae 83, 93
    American 83
    Holmstrup 2
Ash Leaf Spirea 52
Azalea 43, 97
Barberry 14
    Japanese 14, 88, 97
    Korean 14, 89, 97
    Mentor 14, 15
Bittersweet 71, 97
    American 71, 89
    Chinese 71
Boston ivy 74, 96
Box, Boxwood 17
    Dwarf Korean 88
    Korean 17, 93
Bristly Locust 48, 99
Buckthorn 41
    Common 41, 95
    Glossy 41, 97
Buffaloberry 51, 88
    Silver 51, 89, 93
Burning Bush 25, 89, 95
Butterfly Bush 16, 89, 95
Caragana 18
Chokeberry 12, 89
    Black 12, 98
    Purple 12
    Red 12, 88, 98
Coralberry 57, 88, 94
    Chenault 57
    Coralberry 57
Cotoneaster 22
    Cranberry 22
    Hedge 22, 88, 97
    Spreading 22
Creeping mahonia 34, 89, 99
Currant 47
    Alpine 47, 88, 97
    Buffalo or clove 47, 89, 97
Daphne 23, 88, 89
    Burkwood 23, 97
Dogwood 19
    Gray 19, 89, 94
    Pagoda 19, 97
    Redosier 19, 88, 89, 94
    Tatarian 19, 88, 94
Dwarf Arctic Blue Willow 49
Dwarf Bush-honeysuckle 24, 88
Eastern wahoo 25, 89

Elder 50
    European red 50, 96
    Scarlet 50
Elderberry 50, 88
    American 50, 89, 96
Falsespirea
    Ural 99
Fir 93
Forsythia 27, 95
    Golden bells 27
Grapeholly 34, 88
Honeysuckle 32
    Amur 33
    European fly 32, 88, 95
    Hairy 89
    Miniglobe 32
    Sakhalin 32
    Tatarian 32, 88, 89, 95
    Trumpet 72
    Vining 72, 95
    Wild 33
Hummingbird vine 70
Hydrangea 29
    Hills-of-snow 29, 96
    Nikko blue 30
    Panicle 29, 95
Juneberry 10, 89
Juniper 76, 93
    Chinese 76
    Common 76,
    Creeping 76, 88, 89
    Eastern redcedar 76, 89
    Japgarden 76
    Rocky Mountain 76, 89
    Savin 76
Lilac 59
    Chinese 59, 94
    Common 59, 89, 94
    Hyacinth 59, 94
    Late 59, 88, 94
    Littleleaf 59, 94
    Manchurian 59, 94
    Meyer 59, 94
    Preston 59, 94
Mockorange 35, 89
    Lemoine 35
    Lewis 35
    Sweet 35, 96
    Virginal 35
Nannyberry 63, 95

Shrubs for South Dakota